S0-EAK-038

Guideposts Best Loved Stories

A Treasury of Guidance and Hope

Introduction by

Van Varner

A Guideposts Book

The illustrations for "Covered by the Cloud" and "The Church That Wouldn't Die" are by John Thompson. The illustration for "No Such Animal" is by Richard Cowdrey. The illustration for "Three Little Kittens" is by Kim Barnes. The illustration for "Stranger on Our Doorstep" is by Peter Scanlon. The illustration for "Blossoming of the Cross" is by Robert McGinnis. The illustration for "Alone Through the Dark" is by Jenny Tylden-Wright. The illustration for "On the Way to Damascus" is by Brian Ajhar. The illustration for "The Blue Angels" is by Nicholas Gaetano. The illustration for "Five-Fingered Fred" is by Richard Williams. The illustration for "Signs of the Times" is by Peter Siu. The illustration for "Lord, Keep My Kids Safe" is by Tim Jessell. The illustration for "The Boat That Bought Daddy Home" is by Raul Colon.

Designed by Adventure House, NYC
Indexed by Indexing Research, Rochester, NY
Jacket designed by Masoff and Scolnik Design
Printed in the United States of America

Contents

CHAPTER 3: **Mysterious Visitors**

CHAPTER 4: **Back Home**

CHAPTER 5: **Adventures in Faith**

CHAPTER 6: **Witness to Glory**

CHAPTER 7: **Working Relationships**

CHAPTER 8: **Loving Kids**

INTRODUCTION

"A keepsake volume to read at those times you need a spirit-lifting boost or a little extra love and comfort."

That is what *Guideposts* pledged its readers when the first volume of *Best Loved Stories* appeared and I, for one, was eager to accept that pledge. It has been a strange year as I have recovered from a stroke, but a beautiful year in which *Guideposts*, being *Guideposts*, arranged my working days three days a week which allowed me to take Mondays and Fridays for therapy.

Were there times when I needed a "spirit-lifting boost"? You bet there were, and one guess as to where it was found. A *Guideposts* story was always waiting, whether it was one that offered a prayerful promise of hope or a story that simply helped me stop thinking of myself and start thinking of others. It never failed.

Then came the assignment. Elizabeth Gold and I were asked to select and put together the next edition of *Best Loved Stories*. So it meant a lot of soaking in the very thing that I needed. But the best loved stories? We had our favorites but did they represent the most loved? This was the moment in which I felt a special love for Guideposts readers because of the letters they send us. They write asking for prayers or contribute a bit of stray information, and for our purposes, they added the story that moved them the most. And we could choose, too, from the array of *Guideposts* publications—*Angels on Earth*, *Plus*, *Positive Living*, *Guideposts for Kids*, and *Daily Guideposts*. When we decided on the eight categories under which the stories aligned themselves, the readers choices and our own seemed to fall right into place.

Part of the pleasure was seeing old friends appear: John Sherrill with the moment that gave him a new understanding of age; Jeanne

Hill who learned to respect her daughter's "impractical" decision about a home; Ruth Peale liberally giving "Something of Myself." We laughed our way through some very familiar situations, but mostly there were the new friends who make up the major share of authors. Spencer January is one of them telling about a cloud that protected him during a dangerous moment in World War II, and Marion Ash makes Mrs. Totten memorable "as long as the earth endures, seedtime and harvest, cold and heat"(Genesis 8:22). Who says that the *Kids Corner* is only for kids? Try Aline Newman's "education is power" piece. And Shep Varner, how she got in is as mysterious as Laura Curan's "Our Mysterious Man in Bulgaria."

So now Elizabeth and I turn this book to you. It is truly a keepsake volume, one that you can read when you need a spirit-lifting boost, or maybe just a little love and comfort. I know, for I have been there, twice.

—*Van Varner*

Guideposts Best Loved Stories

1

Prayer Really Works

Trouble and perplexity
drive us to prayer,
and prayer driveth away
trouble and perplexity.

— Philipp Melanchthon

COVERED BY THE CLOUD

by Spencer January

It was a morning in early March, 1945, a clear and sunny day. I was 24 years old and a member of the U.S. Army's 35th Infantry Division, 137th Infantry, Company I. Along with several other companies of American troops, we were making our way through dense woods, toward the Rhine River in the German Rhineland. Our objective was to reach and take the town of Ossenberg, where a factory was producing gunpowder and other products for use in the war.

For hours we had pressed through an unrelenting thicket. Shortly after midday word was passed that there was a clearing ahead. At last, we thought, the going would be easier. But then we approached a large stone house, behind which huddled a handful of wounded, bleeding soldiers who had tried to cross the clearing and failed.

Before us stretched at least 200 yards of open ground—bordered on the far side by more thick woods. As the first of us appeared on the edge of the clearing there was an angry rat-tat-tat and a ferocious volley of bullets sent soil spinning as far as we could see. Three nests of German machine guns, spaced 50 yards apart and protected by the crest of a small hill to the left, were firing across the field. As we got our bearings it was determined that the machine guns were so well placed that our weapons couldn't reach them.

To cross that field meant suicide. Yet we had no choice. The Germans had blockaded every other route into the town. In order to move on and secure a victory, we *had* to move forward.

I slumped against a tree, appalled at the grim situation. I thought of home, of my wife and my five-month-old son. I had kissed him good-bye just after he was born. I thought I might never see my family again, and the possibility was overwhelming.

I dropped to my knees. "God," I pleaded desperately, "You've got to do something. Please *do* something."

Moments later the order was given to advance. Grasping my M-1 rifle, I got to my feet and started forward. After reaching the edge of the clearing I took a deep breath. But just before I stepped out from cover, I glanced to the left.

I stopped and stared in amazement. A white cloud—a long fluffy white cloud—had appeared out of nowhere. It dropped from over the trees and covered the area. The Germans' line of fire was obscured by the thick, foggy mist.

All of us bolted into the clearing and raced for our lives. The only sounds were of combat boots thudding against the soft earth as men dashed into the clearing, scrambling to reach the safety of the other side before the mist lifted. With each step the woods opposite came closer and closer. I was almost across! My pulse pounding in my ears, I lunged into the thicket and threw myself behind a tree.

I turned and watched as other soldiers following me dove frantically into the woods, some carrying and dragging the wounded. *This has to be God's doing*, I thought. *I'm going to see what happens now.*

The instant the last man reached safety, the cloud vanished! The day was again clear and bright. *I can't believe this.*

The enemy, apparently thinking we were still pinned down behind the stone house on the other side, must have radioed their artillery. Minutes later the building was blown to bits. But our company was safe and we quickly moved on.

We reached Ossenberg and went on to secure more areas for the Allies. But the image of that cloud was never far from my mind. I had seen the sort of smoke screens that were sometimes set off to obscure troop activity in such a situation. That cloud had been different. It had appeared out of nowhere and saved our lives.

Two weeks later, as we bivouacked in eastern Germany, a letter arrived from my mother back in Dallas. I tore open the envelope eagerly. The letter contained words that sent a shiver down my spine. "You remember Mrs. Tankersly from our church?" my mother wrote.

Who could forget her? I smiled. Everybody called Mrs. Tankersly the prayer warrior. Frankly, I sometimes thought she carried it a bit too far.

"Well," continued my mother, "Mrs. Tankersly telephoned me one morning from the defense plant where she works. She said the Lord had awakened her the night before at one o'clock and told her, 'Spencer January is in serious trouble. Get up *now* and pray for him!'"

My mother went on to explain that Mrs. Tankersly had interceded for me in prayer until six o'clock the next morning, when she had to go to her job. "She told me the last thing she prayed before getting off her knees was this"—here I paused to catch my breath—"'Lord, whatever danger Spencer is in, just cover him with a *cloud*!'"

I sat there for a long time holding the letter in my trembling hands. My mind raced, quickly calculating. Yes, the hours Mrs. Tankersly was praying would have indeed corresponded to the time we were approaching the clearing. And 6:00 A.M.? With a seven-hour time difference, her prayer for a cloud would have been uttered at one o'clock—just the time Company I was getting ready to make its daring dash.

From that moment on, I intensified my prayer life. For the past 52 years I have gotten up early every morning to pray for others. I am convinced there is no substitute for the power of prayer and its ability to comfort and sustain others, even those facing the valley of the shadow of death.

DAY OF PRAYER

by Pam Kidd

"Please, let's not talk about this anymore," I said to my mother. Then I hung up, angry. A relative with a fondness for misery had said some mean, hurtful things to Mother. No matter what kind deed my mother might perform, Aunt Nana will find some way to criticize her. No matter what good thing happens to her, Aunt Nana will find a way to dampen Mother's happiness. "She's not like you," I had said to my mother. "Why can't you shut her out of your life?"

Now, I sought out a comfortable corner of the living room and sat down to pray away my irritation, but no words came. Finally, I settled in reciting the Lord's Prayer: "Our Father," I began.

I imagined a father with his children gathered around him. Some of them loving and kind, others bickering and fighting. Sometimes they even hurt each other. And does the good father love one child more than the other? No. The father loves each of them, even the misery-makers, as if he or she were his only child.

Today has been set aside as the National Day of Prayer, and all around the country, many of God's children are praying, "Our Father." Their differences might frighten, even irritate me. But no matter what their political choices, language or style of dress, all of them, rich and poor, well-educated and unlettered, are praying, "Our Father."

I want to be a part of this day of prayer. I want to pray for understanding, forgiveness and peace. I want to ask our Father to show me how I can love all my brothers and sisters, the way He loves. But, first, I must go back to the beginning.

Down Payment on a Dream

by Leona Karni

My teenage daughters, Sara and Reneé, and I were living on the Eastern Shore of Maryland in the late 1970s. I was a single parent, scraping by on a Social Security disability check. We were grateful for the row house I was able to rent in Chestertown. I had learned how to make ends meet so we had just enough for rent, food, utilities and clothes.

I found it hard, however, to sleep with the noise from the street below my window. I wanted a house of my own, with a room for each girl, trees in front, and peace and quiet. I was new in my faith at the time, but the more I brought this desire of my heart to God, the more it increased. I had never prayed for something so big.

I had never bought a house before, either. I didn't know what steps to take. I did know I would have to be approved for a mortgage, so early in 1980 I called the Farmers Home Administration (FmHA) in Chestertown and inquired about a home loan. When I told the clerk the amount of my monthly check, she responded, "Don't even bother to apply."

Even so, my desire grew. One morning I was sitting at the breakfast table, praying some, thinking some. Absentmindedly, I pulled a cardboard "Bible Promise" out of the plastic loaf-shaped container I had recently started keeping: "Cast thy bread upon the waters," I read, "for thou shalt find it after many days" (Ecclesiastes 11:1). My knowledge of the Bible was virtually nil back then, but it sounded to me as if I should take some action. I grabbed the phone book, looked under "Realtors" and selected one.

"I want to look at houses, and I need to know how to go about buying one," I told the man at the other end of the line. He made an appointment for the next day.

The first place he showed me was a newly renovated row house on the street behind mine. There were three main rooms lined up one behind the other. The dining room and kitchen opened onto a porch. Upstairs were three bedrooms. Trees were visible from every window. The street was quiet. We walked the entire house and the tiny yard. It was perfect. "I could take this house," I mused.

The agent looked at me perplexedly, then smiled. "Somehow this ought to be harder!"

I was not sure what he meant. He locked the house, and we drove back to his office, where he filled out papers. "You'll have to qualify for a loan, of course," he said.

I thought he was simply showing me what would be involved in buying a house like the one I had seen, but a few minutes later he took the papers and escorted me to the senior agent. As I sank into a chair, a thought came to me: *This is the house I have for you.* I was so overwhelmed I almost missed the agent's question: "How much can you put down on this house, Ms. Karni?"

I reached into my purse and pulled out my checkbook. The balance was $1.56. "I can write you a check for a dollar," I said.

The agent shrugged. "Well, we can make a contract binding with a dollar," he said.

As I prepared to sign the papers, which I now realized were a sales contract, the agent told me the house was owned by the town. I would have to be approved as well as find a mortgage. I left the office dazed. *What have I done?*

The next day I went to town hall and filled out the approval-request forms, then went to the FmHA office. *Maybe I'll have better luck in person.* "You'll be called for an interview," a clerk said. I wondered if she had overlooked my income.

Within days I went before a loan counselor. He handed me a sample sheet and said, "Show me how you would budget your monthly income."

I made a list. The gentleman whistled when he saw my numbers. "This is impressive, Ms. Karni! I wouldn't have believed anyone could have made so little go so far!"

During the weeks that followed I went to see the row house every day. "Oh, God, would you?" and thought, *Yes, I really think you will!* I pictured the house wrapping me and the kids in peace. But one day as I stood in the yard, I realized there would be grass to cut and leaves to rake. I had no mower and no rake—yet.

"And I'll need a shed to put them in!" I said aloud. Of course I hadn't a penny in the budget for a shed, but then I had had only one dollar to buy a house . . . .

Six weeks to the day after I called the real-estate agent, I received a call from the mortgage company. I had been approved for a low-interest 30-year loan! My payments would be no more than my current rent.

Next I had to call town hall and see if I had been approved to purchase the house. As I dialed the town manager's office, however, it dawned on me that when someone bought a house there were closing costs.

"Lord . . . ?" It was a partial prayer, as Mr. Ingersoll, the town manager, came on the line. He assured me I had been approved by the town. Almost as an afterthought, he added, "Oh, yes, Ms. Karni, the town had extra money from a restoration grant for the house. We have to use it or lose it, so we'll pay your closing costs. And we had a storage shed built for the backyard. It will be delivered soon."

The real-estate agent seemed surprised but pleased that I had actually found a way to purchase the house. As we finished closing, he handed me a piece of paper from my folder.

"Here, Ms. Karni. Processing a check for a dollar is not cost-effective. You may have it back!"

The next day the girls and I moved in. We had so little, it didn't take us long to get settled. After supper I sat with the girls in our cozy, freshly painted living room and thought about the events of the past few months. I had dreamed of a house of my own and prayed about it. I had pursued my dream and tested my newfound faith, "but God gave the increase" (I Corinthians 3:6). And we were living in our dream house.

Now whenever I have a need I follow the same procedure. Sometimes God's answer is what I expect, sometimes not. Sometimes I get what I want; sometimes I don't. But God has always given the increase when what I want is what I need.

A Tap on the Window

by Suzanne Asplin

Our office is located along a dead-end street. At the very end of that street, there is a single house. That's where Jane and her husband live. One day, I ran into her in the market.

"Hi, Jane. Did you know that our business is now located in the building near your house?" I asked.

"Yes," she replied, "I had heard that."

"I've seen you walk past. Stop in sometime and have a cup of tea with me. I often have free time and would love company."

"Thanks, Sue, I'll do that."

It was just a short exchange and we were soon on our separate ways. I had sincerely meant the invitation; however, I doubted that Jane would ever stop in. We were acquainted through mutual friends, but had never had the opportunity to develop a close friendship, so I knew she would be uncomfortable dropping in at my office.

In the coming weeks, each time I saw her walk past the office, I thought I should go out and ask her to come in, but the time was never just right. Sometimes, I was busy with other people, phone calls, or bookkeeping. At other times, I simply hesitated too long and she had gone past.

One particular day, however, I saw Jane walk past my office window, and a few minutes later, walk back in the other direction. Without conscious effort on my part—almost as though someone else were doing it—I simply tapped on the window and beckoned for her to come in. She didn't even hesitate; just looked up, turned and came in.

I knew there had been many problems and hurts in Jane's life, the most recent being a terrible automobile accident in which her daughter had been seriously injured. A mangled body plus brain damage had kept this young mother hospitalized and comatose for weeks.

After chatting about insignificant matters for a while, I asked how her daughter was doing.

Jane replied, "Alison has made remarkable progress. Her broken bones are mending and she can be up in a wheelchair now. When she came out of the coma, she had the emotional maturity of a two-year-old child, but now has progressed to that of a twelve-year-old. We have reason to expect that she will fully recover. But it is so difficult to deal with a twelve-year-old who is actually twenty-four years old. And Alison's little girl is so confused when her mommy thinks her daughter is a little friend who has come over to play, or when she is 'tired of playing' and wants to send her 'home.'"

When I asked Jane how she was coping with all this, the tears came and Jane began to let all the pent-up feelings pour out—the fear, the grief, the anger, the hurt, the guilt, the frustrations, the fatigue, the financial strain, the doubts, the questioning . . . .

Jane had reached a very low point where she was questioning why God would allow her to go through one heartrending circumstance after another; wondering if she were even worthy of calling herself a Christian—surely a "good Christian" wouldn't have to endure all this testing and trauma. Surely others must look at her and wonder why she and her family had to be "pruned" to this extent, and why they had to walk through one "valley" after another.

Having struggled through some difficult years recently myself, I was able to empathize with Jane and share with her some things that had helped me. But, as always when talking with someone who is hurting, I felt so inadequate, so helpless. I could cry with her, I could listen to her, I could pray for her and her family, but I couldn't take away her hurt or ease her pain.

No, I couldn't, but Someone else could. Someone who knew of her doubts, fears, guilt, anger, hurt and questioning; Someone who knew that she felt He had abandoned her; Someone who knew she needed reassurance that He heard her pleading, saw her tears and loved her.

For, you see, as she was walking—no, she said she was stomping—down the street, she was crying out in her heart to her Lord:

"God, aren't You there anymore?"

"God, how can I go on?"

"God, it is too much and I feel as though You have left me to handle this all by myself!"

"God, don't You love me?"

"God, if You love me and if You are there for me, send someone to help me! Someone that I can talk to! Please, Lord."

"I need someone now!"

And then, at that very moment, she heard a tap on the window.

The Church That Wouldn't Die

by Kay Roberts

You could say our new minister came under false pretenses. Faith United Methodist Church was dying and it was understood he was sent to help merge us with the larger First Methodist Church in town. Our attendance was down, finances were strained, and it didn't make sense to go on any longer.

At one time our little yellow brick church had boasted a sizable congregation. The church was built in 1891—when Neenah was a growing dairy and manufacturing center with large paper mills nearby—but its membership had dwindled. Older parishioners had died off or moved away, and one of the few young families in the church was mine.

I had worked on the committee planning for the merger, and things seemed to be in order. When our minister went to a larger church, his replacement, R. A. Pegram, moved into the parsonage with his wife and five children. Word was soon out that the new pastor—R. A., as he liked to be called—had suffered several heart attacks and that the bishop had sent him here to rest and recuperate until the merger was complete. "We won't see much of him," people said.

But not long after he arrived, R. A. surprised us. Short, balding and middle-aged, he solemnly mounted the pulpit and read from the thirty-seventh chapter of Ezekiel. "The prophet Ezekiel spoke to a valley of dry bones and God raised them up as a mighty army," he said, then paused with a twinkle in his green eyes. "I serve the same God and I will preach until this church is a mighty army marching for him."

A shock wave surged through the congregation. R. A. made it clear that he had not come to close down Faith Church, but to make it grow. "Together we can make a difference," he said. "So it looks like you're stuck with me."

To my surprise I felt a small thrill. It's always exciting to see someone take up a challenge, but privately I wondered if this ailing man was up to the task. Breathing life into dry bones? It would be more like beating a dead horse.

From the first, R. A.'s preaching startled people. He spoke from the Bible and his message was that we must invite Christ into our hearts to be fulfilled. He talked about what the Holy Spirit could do for us. "Too many of us are walking around with this beautiful gift," he said, "but we haven't unwrapped it." He said this meant completely putting our lives in Jesus' hands so we could be everything God intended us to be.

Parishioners had different reactions. "He's talking like one of those Pentecostals," one woman grumped. Another felt he went on too much about the Bible. But R. A. didn't change his message. In weeks to come he stressed the power of prayer and how Christ could heal us of our anxiety and worry. Quoting from the Book of James, he even described the laying on of hands for healing the sick.

After a few months, some longtime members who didn't like his preaching left the church. Despite that, our membership grew. New people, especially younger folks hungry for R. A.'s message, showed up. On Sundays it became harder and harder to find a parking space close to the church.

R. A. had a tremendous amount of energy. To keep in shape he walked everywhere, and he was impossible to keep up with. When he wasn't involved with church business, his hobby was fixing up old Peugeots. He salvaged one for parts and rebuilt another, discarding the chassis in his backyard, what I came to refer to as R.A.'s Peugeot sculpture garden.

In the pulpit he exhibited a wonderful sense of humor. Announcing a hymn, he said, "I want everyone to sing loud and clear." Then he glanced down at my husband, Ron, who can't carry a tune in a bucket, and added, "Except for Ron. You just hum along." He made jokes about his short stature and his baldness ("God has an easy time numbering the hairs on my head") and he surprised people by calling their names in sermons ("God loves you too, Elmer").

He turned out to be a terrific fund-raiser. How he did it was a mystery, because he never once mentioned money in a sermon. "When God called me, we made a deal," he explained. "I said I'd be his servant as long as I didn't have to raise money." Evidently, people gave out of their love of God.

In time the merger committee simply disbanded, and I was attending a regular Bible study instead. I read the Scriptures with more care, applying them to my own life. I found I was coming to know Jesus on a more personal basis than I ever had before.

Then disaster struck. A phone call brought the news. "R. A. has been rushed to the hospital. It's his heart. If he survives, he'll need surgery."

If he survives? I thought. How could we lose our pastor so soon after he had arrived?

My friend Bev Nitschke immediately organized a 24-hour prayer vigil so R. A. would be covered through the night. The next morning she remembered his preaching from James about anointing the sick with oil. She got on the phone and called people to gather at R. A.'s bedside.

That evening six members of the congregation showed up. They stood around R. A.'s bed and read

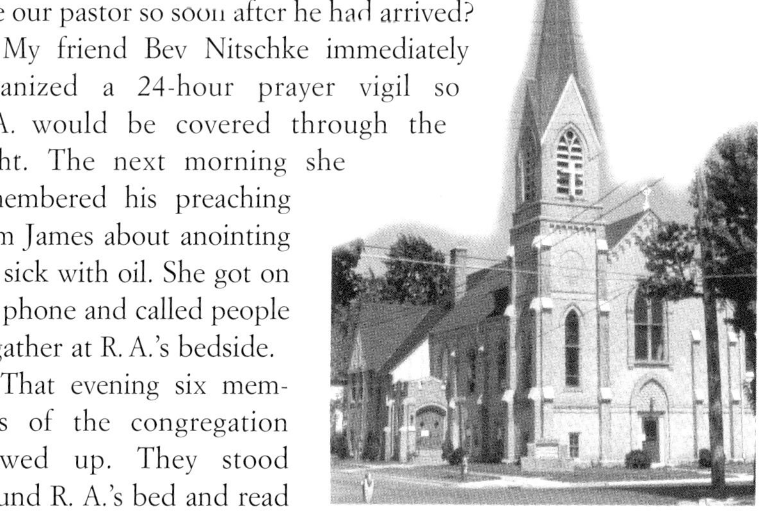

verses of hope and strength. Then they inscribed a cross on his forehead with consecrated oil as each one prayed.

R. A., his face ravaged with pain, managed a weak smile and gasped, "I really appreciate your prayers and feel comforted, but I don't think I've been healed. I still have the pain."

The six, feeling helpless, stood around the bed trying to comfort him and his wife Frances. Then one of the women began to feel a tingling in her hands. She prayed and put her hands on R. A.'s chest. She said it felt like a current passing through them.

"I felt lifted out of my body," R. A. said later. "And I had to remind the Lord I wasn't asking him to take me but to heal me." When the woman removed her hands, R. A. said he knew he had been healed. All the pain was gone.

The next morning he had a scheduled heart catheterization, a procedure in which arteries are explored through X-rays. Afterward his cardiologist sat down with him and Frances and said, "Pastor Pegram, it looks better than we expected."

"What about damage to his heart?" Frances asked the doctor.

"We don't see any," he said.

"How about restrictions?" she pressed.

The doctor said, "He can pretty much do what he wants."

Three weeks later R. A. helped shovel some of the 40 tons of gravel that were used for the foundation of his new home. A sick clergyman had healed a dying church, and in turn the church healed the ailing minister. What an exchange of gifts! Several years later the church burned to the ground, but by that time it was already bursting at the seams. Under R. A.'s leadership we built a new, larger church to hold our expanding congregation, and the mortgage was paid off in record time.

Just before he retired last year, R. A. shared his latest vision for the church. He expects our membership to reach 7000. I wouldn't think it's possible, but over the years I've learned something from R. A. When you believe something and act on it, amazing things can happen. A mighty army can be raised up from a valley of dry bones.

You Can't Out Give God

by Diane Robertson

As an adult disabled with lupus, I live on a limited income. I must maintain close track of my finances, because the money frequently runs out before month's end. I believe in tithing; whatever we give to God, we receive back tenfold. I also believe in positive thinking. Not long ago, I learned a deeper meaning of that term, one I deem will continue to enrich my life.

For the past year, along with volunteering two hours weekly in our church bookstore, I gave what I could afford on Sunday morning. Although committing to a set amount the church could expect to receive monthly, I generally found that on the last Sunday of the month, I had no money to give. I felt badly, but was doing the best I could. After all, I had to eat and, frequently, financial challenges appeared. Whatever the case, I was caught short.

Then one day, I started thinking about my church and tithing, and what they both mean to me. What would I ever do without faith? I want my church to grow and flourish. And God has always been there, never failing me.

Each morning, I prayed, "Dear Father, sometimes anxiety and worry paralyze my spirit. But You have said, 'Fear not.' Please assist me in trusting myself completely to Your healing hands, and to rest in Your great love. Amen."

One day after my prayer, I suddenly understood the magic of tithing. It means "trust," being secure in my faith, affirming in God enough to know that, by believing in Him, He'll support me far above my wildest anticipation. He's not going to let me down.

I decided to experiment. When the next month began, I wrote a check for the entire monthly amount and placed it in the offering. Although I was frightened, I knew God would be there.

Miraculous things happened. A check appeared in the mail—an old friend repaying a loan. A new acquaintance invited me to dinner. Tithing was like a game; the more I gave, the more I received. I found that you can't out give God.

Now I give fearlessly—on the first Sunday of the month—all the money I've committed to my church. I do so joyously, because I know my month is going to be superlative. I trust, even expect, wonderful things to happen. I'm committed to God, and that confidence is reciprocated. This positive thinking really does work!

I've even put the idea to use in other aspects of my life. I ask, "What else do I want more of? Friends? Love?" Whatever, first I must trust enough to give. To have more friends, I must first be a friend. To have more love, I must be more loving. I do this with sincerity and genuineness.

Positive thinking has changed my life.

A Doctor's Boldness

by Stoney Abercrombie, M.D.

The tropical sun beat mercilessly on Yulansoni, a village of mud-brick huts in Tanzania, East Africa. I felt its heat as I stood in shade by the massive 15-foot trunk of a *mbuyu* tree on August 21, 1996. Ten years earlier I had started Volunteers in Medical Missions (VIMM), which now serves poverty-stricken people in 17 countries throughout the world. None were more needy than the hundreds of multitribed villagers who stood before us. A few wore nothing but grass skirts, their earlobes cut according to custom. The bush landscape around us concealed lions, gazelles, monkeys and occasional bandits.

Our team consisted of six doctors, two nurses, two premed students, eight local translators, the local Christian missionary and our bus driver. That day, before beginning our clinic work, I told the story of the Israelites crossing the Red Sea as they fled from the Egyptians. They were saved not by their own power, I explained to the crowd, but by relying on God, who held the waters aside for them so they could cross on dry land.

Midafternoon, as we were working in the hut built for our use as a clinic, people from a village five miles distant carried in a woman too weak to walk. Burning with fever, dehydrated, her black skin paled, she lay on the table, unable to sit up and in obvious pain. The extreme whiteness of her eyes indicated anemia; the distension and rigidity of her abdomen, internal bleeding and infection. A few questions and answers led us to diagnose a ruptured tubal pregnancy.

Under the best of conditions in a modern hospital the woman's chances of survival would not have exceeded 50 percent and would have entailed complications if she did survive. But the nearest hospital was 300 kilometers away.

She was given two liters of intravenous fluid and an injection of antibiotics. There was nothing more we could do for her medically. My clinical judgment told me she would die that night, if not within the next few hours.

I asked the native missionary if he would speak to her in Swahili for me. "Do you know Jesus Christ as your savior?" I asked.

"I've never heard of him," came back the feeble reply.

"May I tell you about him?"

"Yes."

Believe me, I do not usually have such conversations with my patients. Yet I felt an urge to prepare the woman for death. I explained briefly how Jesus came from heaven to love everyone, and how when people die they will go to heaven if they believe he is the Son of God. Through the interpreter I said a prayer that the woman repeated after me: "Please forgive me for anything wrong I have done. I want to live with you in heaven. I realize who you are and I want to be a part of you."

Then an unaccustomed boldness came upon me. Why couldn't we go one step further and believe God could heal her? In the Bible such things happened. Of course, it might not be God's will to heal her, I reasoned, but if it were, what a wonderful way to show the Yulansoni villagers the power of God!

Aloud, through the interpreter and in the hearing of those present, I asked in prayer that if it were God's will, He would heal her.

I'm not sure what I expected to see when I opened my eyes. Unlike people in Bible stories, the woman did not get up from the table and walk. Instead, she continued to lie there helplessly. As tears of compassion rolled down my face, I could only feel I had done what I could to prepare her for death.

We now faced a further problem. We had to start the two-hour ride back to our home base at Singida in order to arrive before nightfall. But the friends who had brought the woman had since returned to their village. Following the only course available, we lifted her into our bus and took her over five miles of bush country to her village, laying her gently on the dirt floor of her mud hut. We told her drunken husband that his wife was very ill and might die, but he received our interpreted message with an equanimity attributable, I thought, either to his state of intoxication or to the low value their culture places on women.

As I sat in the back of the bus on the way to Singida, I quietly communed with God. *Lord,* I prayed, *for your glory, please cure this woman.* Gradually I became infused with an inner peace that told me God was indeed going to heal her. Rising from my seat, I said to the other team members, "I feel in my heart that the woman has been healed!"

Silence. *He's really put his foot in his mouth this time,* I imagined them thinking. Maybe I had. Who was I to think God would perform a miracle just because I had prayed for it?

The next day, we returned to Yulansoni and I asked for news of the woman. Had she died? But since her village lay five miles distant, no one knew. Wednesday, our last day in Yulansoni, I asked again. Still no one had any news. If she had died, the missionary informed me, she would already have been buried, for tropical conditions mandated rapid interment.

Usually mission clinics are noisy. Crowds mill; children cry; doctors, patients and interpreters talk simultaneously. So I felt curiosity and some alarm at midafternoon when a sudden hush interrupted my patient examination. I looked up to see the crowd of people parting like the Red Sea to let a barefoot woman in a handmade, pullover dress pass through.

Afraid to believe, I found myself walking over and putting my arm around her. Through the interpreter I asked, "Are you all right?" Her smile answered me more eloquently than words. She told us she had walked the five miles from her village—with no pain or discomfort. I gave her a thorough examination. Her abdomen had returned to normal. She had no fever. Her healing was complete.

In an awed whisper, one of my colleagues asked, "Our medicines didn't heal her, did they? It was the prayer and a miracle, wasn't it?"

"Yes," I replied, "it was."

The primary directive of Volunteers in Medical Missions indicates that teams must make a difference in the lives of those they visit. This year we are returning to Yulansoni to build a combination medical clinic and church to care for both the physical and spiritual needs of the villagers. We expect to make a difference in their lives—and we are glad to know that once in a while God steps in and makes the difference by Himself.

I Can Hear Him Too

by Carly Dawn Rogers

My older sister Tara and I were both diagnosed with hearing loss when we were children. Surgery helped me get some of my hearing back, but Tara lost all hers. I became my sister's ears. I learned sign language and everywhere we went I was her interpreter.

During the summer after my freshman year in high school Tara and I attended our church's youth camp. We had to rough it: A four-mile hike in the middle of the night was one of the activities. It was a challenge to relay the guide's instructions to Tara by sign in the darkness. But it was all worth it, because we both looked forward to the popular inspirational speaker who was going to address us at the end of the week.

At sunset on our last day, hundreds of us campers rushed toward the arena, jockeying for good seats. Tara and I ended up in the last row, where the sound from the PA system kept fading. I could barely hear the speaker. I glanced at Tara. Tears started to well in my eyes. *My sister will never know what this inspiring man has to say.*

I bowed my head. *God, we need you,* I prayed. I was at the edge of my seat trying to catch even one word. Then suddenly, incredibly, I could hear the speaker's voice loud and clear. I tapped Tara on the shoulder and began to sign furiously. But she stilled my hands and looked at me in amazement.

"Shh, Carly," she whispered. "I can hear him too."

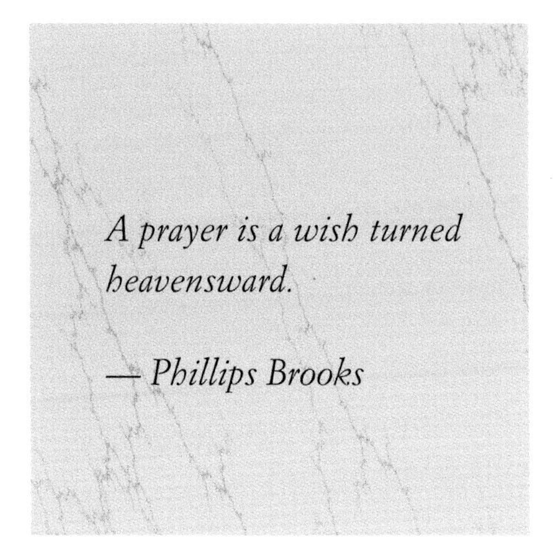

THE WISE GARDENER

by Mary Ruth Howes

The earth is satisfied with the fruit of thy works....
—Psalm 104:13

Almighty God, I pray Thee to help me
to fill up the vacant places in my life.
Thou dost make the odd corners in nature beautiful.
Teach me Thy way, O Lord!
Let me plant flowers in the empty places.
Make the very corners of my life centers of spiritual loveliness.
Make me a wise gardener,
and let my life abound in flowers and fruits.

–J.H. Jowett

I found this prayer for June 30 in a tiny book entitled *The Daily Altar* by J.H. Jowett, published in 1907. The book consists of a brief prayer for every day of the year. Praying that prayer has made me do a lot more thinking about surprises and corners and flowers. Corners have to be empty to be filled. That's why I turn over my garden every year and throw all the dead plants and weeds into the compost.

"But how do we plant flowers in our lives?" I asked my friend Eunice, after I read the prayer to her.

"Create a beautiful memory," she replied after a moment of thought. "Do something nice for someone else. Whenever someone does something nice for me, it creates such a beautiful feeling that I want to do that for someone else.

"And," she added, "for me I think it means not complaining or always focusing on the negatives, but focusing on all the good things in my life and thanking God for them."

Thanks, Eunice, for helping me understand that to be a wise gardener, I must create loveliness for others every chance I get. And I must take time to appreciate the beautiful gifts and people God has put in my life.

O Master Gardener, root out of my life the weeds of complaining and negativity, so that Your loveliness may grow in me and I may pass it on to others.

On the Move!

by Sandra Godfrey

What if your church took off like Noah's Ark, but landed on unfriendly turf? That's what happened in Swan Quarter, North Carolina, in 1876.

Benjamin Credle and the Methodists of Swan Quarter decided to build a church. They picked the highest spot in the heart of town where the church would be safe from flooding.

But when Benjamin and the church people went to buy the land from Sam Sadler, he said, "No! This is my property, and it ain't for sale!"

Disappointed, Ben Credle and his friends built their little wooden church behind the general store, setting it on brick piers to protect it from foul weather.

But the night before the church was to be dedicated, a violent storm squalled into town. Next morning, tidal waves rose so high, they swooshed the little church off its piers and into the road! Alarmed, townspeople watched their little church floating away. *What will happen to it now?* they thought.

But the church seemed to have a mind of its own. Bumping into the general store, it rebounded right and rolled into town. For two city blocks it rollicked along. Then, gliding off its beeline course, it veered left. Finally, it perched on the highest spot in town—right in the middle of Sam Sadler's property!

Sam, seeing the church moved in this mysterious way, thought God might be at work. So he deeded his land to the church.

The congregation named their little church Providence because, they said, providence means "moved by the hand of God."

Today, one hundred and twenty years later, Providence still stands in Swan Quarter, on the highest spot in the heart of town. It reminds folks who hear its story that God provides for His people—and His church.

2

All God's Creatures

And God made the beast of the earth after his kind, cattle after their kind and every thing that creepeth upon the earth after his kind: and God saw that it was good.

— Genesis 1:25

No Such Animal

by Carter Allen

My girlfriend, Dawn, and I stayed out late into the night not long after New Year's Day 1996. It was snowing heavily when we got into my car, and we decided to go only as far as my mother's house, about 10 miles away. I drove slowly, the headlights of my compact boring white tunnels in the swirling flakes.

Around 1:30 A.M., about a half hour after setting out, we turned onto Mom's road in a rural area near the northern Minnesota town of Walker. There were only a couple of dwellings on the two-mile stretch leading to her house, and Mom knew all the comings and goings in this quiet area.

By then the storm had become a raging blizzard. The windshield wipers groaned, protesting the mounting accumulation. Ghostly drifts shrouded the road and I tried to keep the wheel steady. I shifted into low gear and Dawn gasped. "Don't worry," I assured her. "We'll make it."

No sooner had I spoken when we hit a hidden dip. The car lurched sideways and I struggled to regain control as we shot into a ditch. "Hold on," I said. The wheels spun futilely when I pressed the accelerator. We were stuck.

"What now?" Dawn whispered.

"We'll have to shovel our way out as best we can," I said.

I reached onto the floor of the backseat. All I had was a snow-brush. Dawn and I got out. Squinting against the stinging crystals, she wielded the brush and I scooped the white powder with my hands, trying desperately to free up space around the tires. But as fast as we dug, the driving snow relentlessly filled in the gaps.

We looked at each other in desperation. The windchill must have been way below zero, with the gale shrieking off the flat fields bordering the road. Our tennis shoes, jeans, sweaters and jackets were no match for the cold. We climbed back into the car and started the engine to warm up. But in about 15 minutes it died.

"Snow blocking the exhaust," I sighed. We sat quietly for a moment, the howling wind stealing through every possible crack. Thick frost built up on the windows.

Think, I told myself. Mom's house was still a good two miles away, too far to walk in this terrible storm.

"Remember that house about a half-mile back?" I asked Dawn. She nodded. "Maybe we can get help there."

"I can't think of any other way out," she said. "Let's go. It's worth a try."

Again we ventured into the blizzard, which had now become a whiteout, and plodded through knee-deep drifts toward the house. After some 10 yards, I looked back. I couldn't see Dawn. I couldn't see more than five feet.

"Dawn!" I called. "Can you hear me?" Retracing my path, I found her. She looked dazed.

"Thought I was right behind you," she said. She wasn't going to make it. I led her back to the car, settled her in and took off running as fast as I could to the house.

Finally I stomped onto the dark stoop and pounded on the door. After a while a porch light blinked on and a man pulled open the inner door. I saw him pull the screen door shut.

"I'm sorry to wake you," I said, "but my car is stuck in a ditch, and my girlfriend and I are stranded."

"Can't help you," the man said, his face set, and he started to push the door closed. I could see that he was old and frightened, but I tried again. "Please, I just need to use your phone."

"Don't have one," he said. "And my car doesn't work. Like I said, I can't help you." He shut the door. The light went off.

What are we going to do? Tears froze on my face as I headed back to the car. My shoulders and back tense from bracing against the driving snow, I trudged on, feeling weaker with every step. Stumbling along, I was dimly aware of something following me. But I was so exhausted, so agonizingly cold, it was all I could do to put one foot in front of the other. I didn't have the strength even to turn around and investigate. *Too much effort*, I thought sluggishly. "God," I said, "only You can help us now." Then, my head swimming in blackness, I pitched forward into a drift . . . .

When I came to, a prickly, hairy form covered me like a blanket. *What . . . ?* Some sort of a huge black dog was lying on top of me. "Good boy," I whispered, rubbing my hands in the stiff fur under his neck. *Is he wild?* I wondered. *No pet would be out in this weather.* I looked into his eyes. He seemed somehow to *want* to help me, almost as if he *knew* why we had crossed paths.

I pressed my face into his thick fur and breathed the air warmed by his body. The dog stood up.

What a magnificent animal, I thought. I had never seen a similar breed. Feeling new strength, I rose and headed for the car. I half expected the dog to continue on with me, but looking back I saw nothing; my dark rescuer had disappeared into the storm.

I found Dawn shivering. "I didn't have any luck at the house," I told her. "But on the way back, something incredible happened."

We huddled close in the backseat, and I began to describe my encounter with the mysterious black dog. "What was he like?" Dawn asked. "Was he beautiful?" I stretched out the details, making the story last. Just the telling of it warmed me, and I could feel Dawn relax in my arms.

When morning light brightened our snow-covered windows, we heard the roar of a snowplow. Then someone rapped on the glass. The Good Samaritan driver took us to my mother's house. "You were out all night in that awful storm?" Mom said. "God must have been watching over you."

I told her about the black dog who saved my life, and she looked doubtful. "I know my road," she said. "There's no such dog around here."

Then her eyes widened. "But, you know, twice I've seen a black wolf wandering around that very spot—" She stopped. She knew it as well as I did. That dog, or wolf, or whatever it was, wasn't wandering. It had been sent.

Menaced by a Mad Bull

by Gene Fleenor

It was a Sunday afternoon in mid May 1994 when I went to check the herd I keep on a spread just north of town. Normally I loved going over to the farm, especially on a warm spring day. But not that day. Dr. J. Nathan Wilson, who had fused ruptured disks in my back the year before, had just advised me that not only would I have to quit my job and go on disability but that I would have to get someone else to tend my cattle. My back was too fragile for the physical work of cattle ranching. I felt I was losing everything I loved.

My job was supervision officer for Lubbock County, overseeing probationers and helping them adjust to life out of jail. I had been a policeman in Lubbock for five years, and had become a caseworker after getting a degree in religion from Wayland Baptist University. To me this job was the perfect combination of my background in law enforcement and my interest in the ministry. Every time one of my probationers made it on the outside, I felt I was doing God's work. But now I was worried about my future and confused. I could reconcile having to turn over my farm chores or selling the farm. But the doctor said that even sitting for hours in my office chair was bad for my back. If God was using me in my work, why was it being taken from me too?

I stopped my pickup about 250 feet from where the cattle were bunched up. Wearily, I trudged toward the cattle. On the way, about 50 feet from the herd, I noticed the tailgate was open on the livestock trailer I kept in the pasture. I latched it closed, then headed toward the herd again. And then for no apparent reason I went back and opened the tailgate. I felt weird undoing something I had just done, but I shrugged it off.

As usual, the bull came forward to greet me. Like most bulls, he's a little ornery and more than a little stubborn, but he had never given me any trouble. "Hello, bull," I told him, "I guess you've come to get your ears scratched." I obliged and petted him for a bit. "All right, bull, go over to the cattle," I said, waving him away. He shuffled backward and was about to turn and trot off when he bumped hard into a stray cow. She bellowed. Momentarily, he was off balance and startled. Then he looked at me, angry.

He put his head down and started coming at me slowly but deliberately. "Git, bull! Go on. Back!" I told him sternly, shooing him with my arms. He kept coming, then dipped his head low and butted me.

"Doggone, bull! Git; go on!" I backed away and shooed him with my arms again. He butted me and kept advancing. I balled my fist and smacked his nose hard. He just snorted and kept right on shoving and butting me, pushing me about 30 feet past the trailer. I took my eyes off him for a second to calculate how I might make a run for the trailer when he surged at me. His head bashed into my leg just below the knee.

There was a sickening crunch of shattering bone. Pain flamed up my leg to my neck. The blow knocked my hat and glasses off and sprawled me on my back. The bull kept coming at me, pawing and butting. Each time he hit me, my left leg flopped around below the knee. I nearly passed out from the pain. I started clawing my way back toward the trailer.

"Oh, God," I cried out, "help me get away from him!"

Somehow I dragged myself the 30 feet to the trailer. Once there, I couldn't raise myself the foot and a half to get up. When I tried to wrench my body in with my arms, my right shoulder seized in pain. It was as useless as my left leg. Desperately, I lunged at the trailer. Suddenly I was inside! The bull must have caught me just right and flipped me in. If I had left the tailgate latched, I would have been breathing my last about now.

"God," I prayed, "I know You got me to safety in this trailer, but I have to get out of here. You are going to have to get that bull to go somewhere else."

After a time the bull seemed to lose interest and drifted away with the herd. The shattered bones in my lower left leg popped and ground as I shifted my way out of the trailer. Finally I got both legs on the ground, but the pain was so intense I couldn't edge my way out. "Lord, you are going to have to do it. I can't."

Suddenly I was flat on my back. Two hundred feet of bumpy pasture separated me from my truck. Lying on my left side I was able to inch along, crabbing with my shoulder and pushing with my right leg. I made it about 25 feet and felt exhausted. My shoulder was on fire with pain, and my leg was throbbing.

"God," I said again, "I can't make it. You're going to have to send someone to help me."

A voice played in my mind: *Who do you think you're talking to?* It was not audible, but it was plain as day that God had spoken to me—not loud or angry, but commanding.

Taken aback with fear and wonder, I answered, "I'm talking to You, God. I can't make it without someone's help."

I am here.

I got the message. I began crabbing along again, stopping every five feet or so to rest. Each time I paused I heard, *I am with you.* With endurance beyond my own, I finally scooted under the fence to the pickup. I stared at the door handle. From where I was lying in the dirt road's ruts, it looked a mile high. I twisted my back up against the side of the truck, but when my hand grasped the handle I couldn't open the door because all my weight was leaning against it. If I fell, I knew I would pass out from the pain. "Oh, God, I've got to get this door open some way."

Next thing I knew I was leaning against the truck's seat with the door open. I got inside, but I couldn't drag my left leg in. I put the truck in gear and slowly drove to the nearest neighbor's house, keeping the door open with my left hand and steering with my right. I began to lose consciousness. I pulled up near the neighbor's front door and leaned on the horn, but no one came.

I had to get myself to the hospital, 15 miles away.

I managed to reach the seat release lever and push the seat back. I inched my bad leg in and fastened my seat belt to keep myself upright. I don't remember much about the trip to the hospital except that underlying the terrible pain there was an assurance that came from beyond: *I am in control.* The truck stopped a time or two at lights, then made a U-turn to get on the access road to Saint Mary Hospital. I believe the Holy Spirit was driving that truck more than I was.

Two men standing outside alerted the emergency room staff. After I was on a gurney and being wheeled in, I let myself sink below the haze of pain into unconsciousness.

The next days passed in a blur of numbed pain. On Tuesday Dr. Wilson pieced my shattered leg back together with a metal plate and 20 screws. When I came to after the operation, I felt strange.

That Thursday when my wife, Nita, came to visit, I was picking at my lunch. I told her, "I should be happy just to be alive and that Dr. Wilson saved my leg, but I feel so out of kilter."

"Well, you do have a lot to be thankful for, you—" Nita began.

I felt like I had been hit by a lightning bolt. Suddenly I was back in the pasture latching the trailer tailgate and heading toward the herd. Then I felt the same weird nudge that made me go back and unlatch the tailgate—the nudge that saved my life.

"That's it!" I fairly shouted. "Nita, I left God back in the pickup truck when I got to the hospital. I haven't been listening for Him and I haven't been thankful. That's what's been the matter with me these past few days." Right then I started to pray, "Lord, I'll never leave You out of my life like that."

Immediately I felt right.

Sure enough, I had to go on disability and get out of cattle farming. I needed three more surgeries after that first one to get my leg and shoulder right. Even now I'm not able to move around much. I can sit and stand only for short periods of time. But there is peace in my heart. I have learned to trust God in all things. I used to pray, "This is what I want, Lord, please bless it." Now I say, "Your will, not mine."

Then I put my mind at ease. If God can remove me from the path of an angry bull, then I don't need to worry about tomorrow. God will take care of all my tomorrows in His own perfect way.

Following Mama Cat

by Cleveland S. Baker

I'm a cat person from way back. In 1931, when I was eight years old, I lived with my grandparents on a tobacco and cotton farm in South Carolina. There was no one my age for company, so my best friend was a lovable solid-grey cat, known simply as Mama Cat. I would have been lonely without Mama Cat, and I loved her as much, I imagined, as she loved her two kittens.

The farm was located on a dirt road, and that year the state highway department began expanding it to become part of U.S. Highway 301. The tough work was done by mules towing large shovel-like devices. My grandfather gave the highway department permission to dig a huge well on his property to provide water for the animals. It was four times larger than an average farm well, and sat adjacent to the barn where the tobacco was dried. Granddaddy told me to be careful when I worked around it.

My job was to help bring the tobacco in from the fields and ready the leaves for drying in the barn. My hands would quickly become coated with a black tarry substance—probably one reason I have never smoked.

After the harvest was complete, there wasn't much to do while the leaves dried, which took almost a week. On one of the off days, Mama Cat and her kittens were nowhere to be found. I was disappointed. A short time later I had the strangest urge to take a walk in the field next to the barn, not something I usually did. To me, the tobacco field meant work. I was more content wandering the nearby swamp, rattlesnakes and water moccasins notwithstanding. But this day the tobacco field beckoned irresistibly.

As I stepped among the stripped tobacco stalks, Mama Cat suddenly ran toward me meowing loudly. Then she darted in the opposite direction, looking back as if she wanted me to follow her, which I did. She led me directly to the well. Afraid to look inside the dank, dark pit, I asked God not to let me find anything too scary. Holding on, I peered over the edge. The kittens! They were trapped on a bank of dirt surrounding the water at the bottom. I immediately summoned Granddaddy, and my playmates were rescued unharmed.

Was it an angel's silent urgings that persuaded me to take a walk in the tobacco field? Mama Cat would never have come to me near the swamp, which was much too dangerous for my four-footed friend. In the years since, I have known and loved many cats, but none ever displayed the behavior of Mama Cat that day. Maybe the same angel that persuaded me persuaded her too.

"Ten Minutes from Death," Woman Discovered by Dog

by David Talbot

Gale Coleman, a 43-year-old nanny who lives alone in Cambridge, Massachusetts, was settling in to watch "60 Minutes" during the Blizzard of '96, when she noticed the porch light flickering.

Wearing only a cotton nightgown and robe, Gale walked out onto the porch and climbed up onto a railing to tighten the bulb. The bulb shocked her, causing Gale to let go of the beam she was holding. She fell ten feet into a hard-packed snowbank, cracking two ribs.

For the next 40 minutes, Gale lay helpless, her bruised body barely visible above the snowbank in the alley between two houses. The snow continued to fall, temperatures plunged into the teens, and a strong wind blew. Her screams for help went unheeded.

Gale was almost asleep and near death by the time her neighbor, Randy Foley, arrived home. When Foley let his year-old Great Dane, Kayla, out the back door, the dog ran to the fence that surrounded the house next door and barked frantically. Then, for the first time ever, Kayla howled. Realizing that something was up, Foley let Kayla into his neighbor's yard. The dog immediately started digging in the snowbank.

All of a sudden, Foley saw auburn hair sticking out of the snow. He began scraping snow off the woman's motionless body. An icy sheet covered her face. Beneath that, her skin was gray.

After making a quick trip to his house, Foley wrapped Gale in two comforters and stayed on his cellular phone with a 911 operator until an ambulance arrived.

The EMTs estimated that when Kayla found her, Gale Coleman was within ten minutes of dying.

After two days in a hospital, Gale was able to thank the heroic dog with a hug and a big bone.

Foley believes that the rescue was divinely inspired. He had been at his brother's watching a football game on television and had left before it was over. And he had let Kayla out the back door, not the front as he usually did. "Someone guided me," Foley says. "I believe it was the Lord."

Three Little Kittens

by Phyllis Hobe

In my rural area I often see barn cats hunting in the fields. In exchange for keeping the rodent population down, they get food and shelter from farmers, but they aren't comfortable with people. If they wander onto my property, they run off as soon as they see me.

One morning, however, I found a cat curled up beneath the shrubs in front of my house. It was pregnant, a pretty little gray cat with black stripes. I brought out some food, which the cat gobbled up. She let me pet her and rubbed against me, purring. This was no barn cat. It was a family pet.

I called everyone in my neighborhood, but no one reported a missing cat. I tried the local police, the animal shelter, several veterinarians—with no success. It seemed probable she had been abandoned by her owners. It also was obvious that she was going to deliver her kittens very soon.

What was I to do? I couldn't bring her into my home because she might be diseased. But it was October, and though the days were warm, the nights were cold. At sunset she let me pick her up and I took her into my garage. She curled up on a pile of old towels and at that moment she went into labor.

For the next few hours I watched in awe as the cat delivered three kittens. From what I could see they were not only alive, but vigorous. "As soon as you can, start picking them up and petting them," my veterinarian said when I called him. "That way, when you want to find homes for them they'll be ready to live with people."

Find homes for three kittens? I hadn't thought of that. I called the animal shelter, but I was told if I brought them in they would have to be put to sleep immediately. "It's the way it is," the woman told me. "The newborns and mother might have diseases our other animals could catch." There was a sadness in her voice. "If you can keep them for six weeks, when they finish nursing we can take them in then."

Six weeks, I thought. *But maybe I can find them homes before that.*

My house isn't large and I already had two cats and one dog, so I carried the mother and her kittens down to the basement and piled newspapers and old towels in a box for a nesting place. Of course, my other animals were curious, and it took some athletic maneuvering to get past them every time I used the basement door.

"Lord, I've got six weeks," I prayed. "I need all the help You can give me." I called everyone I knew and passed the word. I ran an ad in the local paper. I even told people I didn't know well and asked them to tell their friends. I kept getting the same response: People who loved cats already had one or more. *Surely*, I told myself, *someone will come forward.*

No one did. As the weeks passed I felt uneasy. Was God going to abandon the animals just the way some human had? I couldn't believe that. But the kittens—two females and a male—were getting bigger, learning how to jump and climb, and I couldn't keep them in the basement much longer. My veterinarian examined them and gave them rabies shots, so I knew they were healthy.

But when I called the animal shelter they had bad news for me. They were overwhelmed with kittens; they couldn't promise to keep them for long. *I can't let them be put to sleep.*

On the last day of the sixth week I reminded God that we had come to our deadline yet nothing was happening. And then it hit me: I had given God an ultimatum. I had more or less told Him I would have faith in Him for six weeks and no more.

I was so ashamed. "Forgive me, Lord," I prayed. "I know You

will help me find homes for these little ones. However long it takes, I'll look after them."

A sense of peace came over me. For the first time I allowed the kittens and their mother to follow me upstairs. I trusted my very friendly dog and cats to accept them, and after a bit of curious sniffing they did.

When the kittens were eight weeks old a friend of a friend called and asked if she could see them. When she did, she fell in love with them and took one of the females home with her. Two days later I had a call from a young couple whose cat had died a month earlier. "We miss him so much," the woman said. They took the rambunctious young male with them. By the next week the third kitten went home with the young man who delivers my fuel oil.

That left the mother cat, whom I decided to keep. Like my animals, she wasn't young and spent most of her time sleeping. But then I had a call from a friend's neighbor. "I'm getting on in years and so is my cat," the woman told me. "We need some company but neither of us can keep up with a kitten. I was wondering if you would let me have the mother."

These events happened three years ago, and all four cats are doing well. As for me, I learned a valuable lesson. Now when I need God's help I simply ask, knowing He will come to my aid. And I don't give Him a deadline.

Miss Hedberg's Homework

by Lou Dean Jacobs

The same week that Miss Hedberg, our new teacher, arrived at school, I began sneaking out of my home at night. I would wait until Sis lay in a lump with the pillow over her head. When the arguing between my parents erupted from the front room, my dog, Shorty, knew the time was right. He'd scratch below my window and I'd slowly unlatch the screen. Dragging Grandma's worn quilt behind me, I'd walk to the willow tree near the creek and lie down under its branches. Shorty would cuddle by my neck all night. Then he'd wake me at first light so I could return to my bed.

Miss Hedberg didn't intrude in our lives the way some other teachers had. Her roots ran deep, back to the time her father had staked a claim to a farm near Kildare, Oklahoma, in 1893. She was country and understood the importance of private things. Yet she had an uncanny ability to zero in on our individual talents and weaknesses. When she realized I was a reader, she began to bring me wonderful treasures from her own library and casually mention they were loaners. Instead of ridiculing me for my math deficiency, she offered a daily review.

One afternoon she caught me on the school steps, scribbling in a notebook that was my diary, while everyone else played crack-the-whip in the playground. I covered the words with my hands and felt my face blush. Miss Hedberg quickly walked on. The next day she happened to tell us about Anne Frank and the seemingly insignificant journal that became a classic.

The word *divorce* boomeranged off the walls of our house one day and I quickly ran to the fat dictionary: "To end marriage . . . to terminate . . . to dissolve." The words sparked a terror in my chest so intense I couldn't breathe.

"I hope they do divorce," Sis said, with her smug teenage smirk. "I'm sick of their fighting."

I dived into her with both hands, yanking her hair and spitting out my anger until she plastered me with a right hook.

Mama announced her departure one morning late in the fall of 1957, just before Sis and I started off across the terraces to school. I stayed with Shorty in the corner of our field until the last bell rang. I made him promise to wait for me, then I bolted across the road into the redbrick building.

Every few minutes during first period I broke my pencil lead so I could go near the window and use the sharpener. I craned my neck around to see if Shorty was still in the field, if Mama's brown station wagon was still in the drive.

When her car disappeared past the schoolhouse in a cloud of red dust, I dropped my pencil and burst through the old wooden doors. I ran toward the corner of the school yard, calling for my dog. When the spotted head popped up in the tall grass, I wailed, and Shorty sprang to his feet and ran to me. I picked him up and carried him to the school steps.

Before long, Miss Hedberg joined me. We sat for a while in the warm breeze.

"You know," she said, "I've been thinking. That dog of yours comes to school every single day. If he's going to be here, he might as well learn something."

Shorty lay obediently by my desk for the rest of the day. During last period Miss Hedberg made an announcement: "Class, we have a new student. Shorty Jacobs, first grade, born right here in Osage County."

So Shorty became a permanent member of Braden School.

Sometimes he'd go quickly to the big wooden doors, tail wagging, and look back. I'd glance at Miss Hedberg for permission. "Yes, you may be excused, Shorty," she would say, looking up from the blackboard. When he returned and gave his "Errff" she stopped writing on the board and allowed one of us to let her "little canine boy" return to class.

Shorty and I graduated from Braden School together, and because Miss Hedberg emphasized the importance of an education, we proceeded to high school and then college. My terrier friend lived to the record age of twenty, seeing me through my childhood and youth.

Miss Hedberg still lives on her father's homestead in Kildare. She will turn ninety-three in April of this year. Last fall the two of us were reunited at the first-ever Braden School Reunion. We shared memories from the blackboard to the outhouse, our heads together like teenage girls at a slumber party.

When it was time for her to go, she trudged with her walker to the schoolhouse windows and looked down at my family's old farm.

"It's been nearly forty years," she said, "but I can still see you coming up over those terraces with Shorty's brown and white spots at your heels." She gave a sly grin. "He was your angel, you know."

"And," I said, sliding an arm around her stooped shoulders, "you think it was only coincidence that you came to Braden School in 1957?"

Her grin stretched into a wide smile. "When you've lived as long as I have, you don't believe in coincidence too much."

When we parted, Miss Hedberg and I exchanged addresses instead of tears. I said a silent prayer, asking God to send more angels in the form of teachers: friends of troubled children who can alter a destiny by putting love at the top of the curriculum.

Home

by Van Varner

Two are better than one....
—Ecclesiastes 4:9

My name is Shep. I am a Belgian shepherd, expected to herd sheep, but in the year and a half of my life I haven't seen any. You see, I've had trouble finding a home. First there was Heidi, who turned me over to a couple in New York City, but when the woman had a baby I went to Betty Kelly to await adoption. *Why didn't they want to keep me?* I was nervous when I was told a man was coming to look at me. *Suppose I didn't measure up? Suppose I didn't like him?* And then Van arrived and, in an instant, none of the worries mattered. I bounded to him and he took me in his arms and I knew that I was his.

So another New York apartment. Very cozy. We got right into a routine: Up at five, he fixes my breakfast at the same time as he does his, then forty-five minutes in Central Park where he unleashes me, but I keep an eye on him as I scurry around. There are more walks during the day, but outside the dog run, the rest are on the leash. I've heard from country and even suburban dogs visiting the park that I was lucky to have so much freedom. I don't know, but who cares? I am with him.

Van hasn't had a dog since his pointer, Clay. Ten years. Imagine going so long. But I have inherited Clay's leash and bowl and have tried in every way to be a worthy replacement. Sometimes I feel I am better, since I do not shed the way he did and I have a more beautiful tail. Yesterday Van took my head in his hands and spoke to me.

"You know, Shep," he said, "God's wisdom is phenomenal. I don't know why He formed this alliance between man and dogs, but I am awfully glad He did. I've been lonely. I've missed a wagging tail when I come home and the regimen you bring to my life. You and I are partners, yes?"

I gave him a big, fat lick.

Van's God, Whoever, wherever You are, thank You.

RIDING INTO THE PAST

by Barbara L. Weber

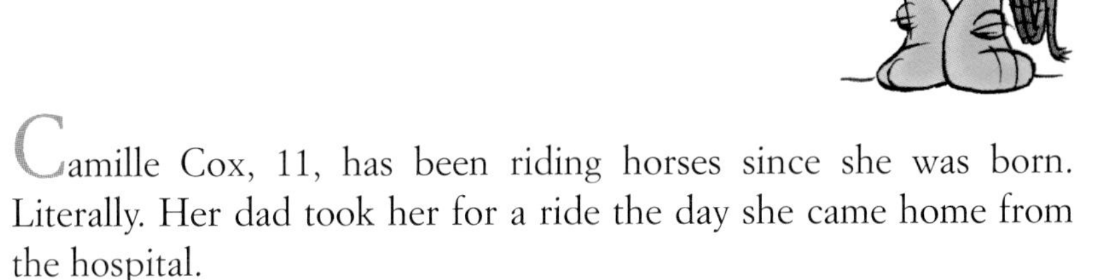

Camille Cox, 11, has been riding horses since she was born. Literally. Her dad took her for a ride the day she came home from the hospital.

Last year Camille and her dad went riding together again. They were chosen to be "outriders," or cowboys, for a special week-long cattle drive celebrating Florida's 150th anniversary as a state. The drive was more than three hundred miles long and included over 1,000 cattle.

Talk about a history lesson! The fourth grader and her horse (she owns three) had to cross creeks. And at night she had to bathe in those same creeks. It was very cold. But she thought the trip well worth it. And now she knows what she wants to be when she grows up.

"I want to be a vet and a farrier (a person who shoes horses) and ride in the rodeo," Camille says. And her love of horses can help her do all three.

3

Mysterious Visitors

Be not forgetful to entertain strangers; for thereby some have entertained angels unawares.

— Hebrews 13:2

Stranger on Our Doorstep

by Arthur Best

The old country doctor set his black bag on the bedside table. "I'm sorry, ma'am," he said. "I'm afraid your boy isn't going to make it through the night. A blue baby, and a month and a half premature, at that. . . . " His words trailed off.

Exhausted from the difficult birth, Garnet nodded and leaned back against her pillows. Compared to her older sons and daughter, who had been sturdy newborns, this baby looked frail and helpless. Garnet knew the boy's chances were slim at best. Besides, if an emergency arose, she and her husband Elmer wouldn't be able to get medical help fast enough, living as they did up a hollow several miles from the nearest town. Their farm lay along a creek, and the only way coming or going was a dusty dirt road.

The doctor cleared his throat. "I have to take your baby with me," he said. "The next twenty-four hours are critical. If he makes it, I'll bring him back tomorrow afternoon." The doctor picked up the baby and carefully settled him inside the black medical bag.

Garnet bit her lip, watching her boy being swallowed up by the worn leather satchel, tiny as he was. "Thank you, doctor," she said, the softness of her voice matching the quiet of that spring day in 1933. "We're grateful."

Elmer saw the doctor to the door, then returned to his wife's bedside. "Doc will take good care of him," he told her. He held her hand, his work-roughened fingers gently curling around hers. "All we can do is pray."

"I know," she whispered, her eyes half closed. "I already am. . . ." She drifted off to sleep.

The next day the whole family—Garnet, Elmer and their three older children—anxiously awaited the good doctor's arrival. Garnet napped fitfully, her thoughts constantly returning to her sickly baby. When a knock finally came at the door, Elmer ran to open it.

"Your boy survived the night," the doctor said, "although I can't quite say how." He lifted the baby out of his bag and placed the tiny bundle in Garnet's arms. The boy still looked alarmingly small, but at least he had a little color.

"Get some milk in him," the doctor instructed. "And keep him warm. He seems to be allergic to cow's milk, but you shouldn't have any trouble if you nurse him." Garnet nodded, feeling reassured.

Not long after the doctor left, the baby awakened with a weak mew. "Are you hungry?" Garnet murmured, and began to nurse him. She was glad to see he had a healthy appetite.

He drank his fill and nodded off, seemingly content. But before long, he began to bawl. "What's the matter, little one?" Garnet asked, gently rubbing his back. The baby promptly spit up nearly all he had consumed. *Maybe he drank too fast*, she thought. *I'll make sure he takes it slower next time.*

The next time—in fact, every time—she nursed him, however, produced the same dreadful results. By nightfall, she was desperate. "He's never going to get stronger if he can't hold his milk down," she told her husband. Remembering the doctor's admonition to keep the baby warm, she put him in a woven basket, blanket and all, and slipped him under the toasty cookstove.

The following day brought no change in the baby. Garnet continued to feed him, hoping he'd keep enough in his stomach for nourishment. By late afternoon, he was whimpering constantly, whether from hunger or from illness, Garnet couldn't tell. She and her husband agreed: It was time to find the doctor.

As Elmer laced up his boots, a faint knock came at the door. Had the doctor decided to stop by? Eagerly Elmer flung the door open. "Doc, we were just—" He stopped short, surprised, when he saw the stranger standing there.

Unfamiliar people had stopped on their doorstep before. During those hard times, folks were walking around everywhere, looking for work in exchange for a hot meal and a place to sleep.

But this woman was different. She was black. In this area of southeastern Ohio, there were very few black people, and they always kept to themselves.

"Do you think you could let me have something to eat," she asked, "and maybe a place to stay? It'll only be until I get my strength back. I had a baby yesterday, and I'm just too tired to go on." When she saw the question in Elmer's expression, she added, "My child was stillborn."

"I'm sorry," Elmer replied, beckoning her in. He led her to the rocking chair in front of the stove, where his wife sat trying to soothe the baby. "I'm Elmer Best, and this is my wife, Garnet. Garnet, this is . . . "

"Jane. Just call me Jane," the woman said. "I promise I'll earn my keep."

"Now I've got to fetch the doctor," Elmer said. "My wife will show you where you can stay." He hurried out, and Garnet explained the situation with the baby.

"I can see you have your hands full," Jane said, gazing sympathetically at the boy in Garnet's arms. "Let me get supper on." While Garnet sat in the rocking chair, desperately trying to quiet her newborn, Jane slowly and methodically fixed a pot of soup from beef bones and vegetables.

By the time Elmer returned, the children had all been fed. "Doc's over in the next county on an emergency," he said, crestfallen. "He won't be back until tomorrow at the earliest."

"Don't worry," Jane said. "I have the feeling your boy will be all right."

After settling the baby in for the night, in his makeshift cradle under the stove, Garnet went to sleep, prayers swirling in her mind. *Lord, please help our child*, she pleaded. *Show us what he needs.*

She awoke feeling more hopeful. When she peeked in the basket to say good morning to their boy, it was empty. In a panic, she yelled for her husband. Their baby wasn't anyplace in sight. Neither was Jane.

"I'm going to check the property," Elmer said, trying to stay calm.

Garnet waited and paced by the stove. Why had they helped this woman? What if she'd run away with their baby? Finally Garnet heard her husband calling from the distance, "I found them!" She raced to the door, relieved to see Elmer with the baby.

"I found them in one of the outbuildings," he explained. "She was letting him nurse from her and hid because she wasn't sure how we would react."

Garnet took her son in her arms and held him close. "Look, Elmer," she said slowly, "her milk seems to agree with him." It was true: The baby was sleeping peacefully, no crying, no spitting up.

Elmer went to get Jane. After she returned to the house, the three of them agreed on the arrangement and didn't speak of the incident again. Nor did they discuss when Jane would leave. Instead she became, in a way, part of the family.

Soon Elmer was back on the job cutting timber, and the two women were busy running the household. Jane never talked much, especially about herself, and Garnet wasn't one to pry. The infant grew slowly but steadily.

One morning Garnet and Elmer arose, expecting Jane's good morning at breakfast as usual. When she wasn't at the stove, Elmer went to see if she was ill. But her bed hadn't been slept in, and her few possessions were nowhere to be found. She wasn't in the garden or anywhere else on their property.

Elmer rushed to their neighbors' place down the creek and asked if they'd seen her. No one had. Not so much as a dog had barked to announce someone passing. He got to thinking, *Did anyone even see her when she came to us?*

When he asked, the neighbors looked bewildered. A black woman wandering these parts would have been noticed, they assured him. The folks at the other farms Jane would have passed on the dirt road to their house didn't know what Elmer was talking about either.

In the months that followed, he and Garnet even asked friends in other counties if they had seen a woman fitting Jane's description.

The answer was always no. It was as if the earth gave birth to her and when she left, the earth swallowed her up again.

Garnet and Elmer were practical folk, with their feet firmly planted on the ground, and they didn't spend a lot of time pondering the mystery of Jane's visit. But whenever they spoke of her, their eyes filled with wonder. I should know. I was that sickly baby boy, and I often heard the story of how a stranger arrived from nowhere to give me the nourishment that only she could give.

Preacher Jake and the Mysterious Note

by Ellen Fackler Gamrath

Twenty-one-year-old John Jacob Trinklein rode his quarter horse across the dusty, lonely north Texas prairie. "C'mon boy!" Trinklein urged, digging his spurs into the animal's flanks. "Giddyap!" The early afternoon sun was strong. Sweat rolled off the young man's forehead and dirt dried his throat. He had miles to go before reaching Honey Grove. Folks there were waiting.

It was 1881, and Trinklein, a Lutheran preacher, had volunteered to become one of the area's first circuit riders for his church. "Preacher Jake," as he was known, was assigned to keep watch over seven widely separated parishes, a territory covering 3600 square miles.

"Yah!"

His horse's pace quickened and thick clouds of dust rose from the parched earth. When the preacher finally reached Honey Grove he headed toward an open field where a dozen or so people had assembled under the shade of a big sycamore for Sunday worship.

The preacher dismounted, wiped his brow with a bandanna and unwrapped his silver communion cup from the velvet pouch he kept it in. "We gather here on God's great land to give him thanks," he began. The sound of hoofbeats interrupted his words. A man on horseback appeared on the horizon. He rode up to the pastor, waving a piece of paper.

"Preacher, you're needed right quick in Choctaw Creek," the man said. Preacher Jake unfolded the note: "George Schultz fell from horse. Dying. Wants last communion." The Schultz homestead was almost thirty miles away. It would take at least seven hours to get there. "I'm sorry, friends, but I must leave now," he told the congregation, and hastily packed up the communion cup. He jumped back in his saddle and was off for yet another long, lonely ride across the prairie.

Dusk slipped into darkness and the full moon lit his path through the mesquite. But for the small storm of dust kicked up by his horse's hooves, nothing stirred the night air.

When he arrived at the Schultz homestead, the cabin was dark. Fearing that George had already passed away, Preacher Jake tapped gently on the door. A dog yapped, and seconds later the rancher's wife Rose answered.

"Landsakes, Preacher Jake!"

"I'm sorry, ma'am," he said, removing his hat. "I only hope I'm not too late."

"Late?" the wife asked, clutching a shawl around the shoulders of her nightdress. "For what?"

The preacher heard footsteps, and out walked George Schultz, healthy as a mule. "What's all the racket?"

"Praise God, man!" the preacher exclaimed. "You're not dying!"

"Dyin'? Why I ain't been sick a day in my life," the rancher declared.

"But the note I got . . . ." The preacher handed the worn piece of paper to the couple.

"Who would play such a hoax?" asked Rose.

"I don't know, ma'am. But all that matters is your husband's fine," the preacher said.

That night he slept in the Schultzes' barn. Up at the crack of dawn, he set out to recruit volunteers to help build a church in one of his parishes. With so much to do Preacher Jake soon forgot about the bogus note.

Days later the preacher got word that one of his parishioners had been jailed for a shooting during a dispute over cattle. In the next few months he made periodic visits to the man in prison, where he found a whole new congregation. Preacher Jake began leading services there. During one visit he was asked to see the men on death row individually, since they weren't allowed to attend the group worship. Preacher Jake followed the sheriff to the cell of Juan Garcia, who was about to be hanged for murder.

"Juan Garcia, the padre is here to see you," the sheriff said.

"Is there anyone you would like us to notify?" the preacher asked.

Juan stared at him intently, but didn't respond.

"Do you have any special requests?" the preacher tried again. Still no answer. He told the prisoner about the thief who hung on the cross next to Jesus and entered paradise with him. "God's merciful love is for everyone," he said. "His forgiveness is there for you too."

"But what if I had killed you?" Juan blurted out. "Would you still believe that?"

"Yes," the preacher said. "God's forgiveness is unconditional."

"Well, Preacher Jake, it *would* have been you—if someone hadn't tipped you off."

The preacher looked at Juan. What was he talking about?

"My partner and I lured you to the Schultz ranch with a fake note. We were going to kill you and steal your horse and the silver communion cup. But we couldn't because of the two men riding with you."

Juan told how the brilliant moon that night gave him a clear view of two riders with shotguns flanking the preacher. But he was confused, he said, about one thing. "Your horse kicked up clouds of dust, but the dirt underneath the other riders was undisturbed. It didn't make sense."

It didn't make sense to me either when as a girl of five or six I first heard the story. You see, John Jacob Trinklein was my grandfather. He lived with us. I loved to sit with him in his dark, book-lined study and listen to him tell about his adventures as a circuit rider. He often made pencil sketches of the places he'd been and the tools he'd used. When he told the story of Juan Garcia and the mysterious note, he even drew the Schultzes' dog, who'd yapped so loudly when he finally reached their cabin on that fateful night.

"Who do you think those two riders were?" I asked Grandpa.

"I was riding solo that night. I know that for sure. I also know I had God's protection. Men facing the gallows don't have reason to lie."

We headed downstairs for supper. The blustering wind rattled the windows and moaned down the chimney, invisible but powerfully real. As I got older Grandpa's story opened up to me possibilities beyond my senses. I wondered what form the angels that had helped him would take in my own life.

The American Character

by Coryne Wong-Collinsworth

It was five days before Christmas. I was 3000 miles from my family in Hawaii, studying to become a nurse. I attended classes all day and then went straight to my job as a waitress. I was homesick, but couldn't afford to fly home for the holidays.

When one of the other waitresses went on break, she asked me to cover for her. "By the way, the guy at table five has been sitting there for an hour," she said. "It's like he's waiting for somebody."

I looked over. There was a slim, pleasant-looking man in worn Levi's, red-and-black plaid shirt and black baseball cap. I went over. "I'm Cory," I said. "Please let me know if you want anything."

"I'd like nachos," he replied.

Nachos were the cheapest thing on the menu. Maybe this guy was broke. I tried my best to make him feel okay. "Coming right up," I said. I returned a few minutes later and slid the nachos in front of him. "That will be two dollars and ninety-five cents."

He handed me a single bill. "Keep the change."

I looked—then looked again. "Excuse me, sir, but you just gave me a hundred-dollar bill."

"I know," he said gently. "Merry Christmas." Then he stood and moved toward the door. I turned to thank him, but he was gone.

After work, I returned to my apartment and was turning on the television when the phone rang. It was my mother. She told me that my brothers had bought an airline ticket to get me home for Christmas, but they could only afford the fare one way. "Can you manage the other part?" she asked.

At that moment, a commercial flashed on the television. A major airline was offering a one-way fare to Hawaii for $99! I jumped off the sofa, shouting, "Thank you, God. I'm going home!"

That was seven years ago. Every Christmas, my husband and I try to do something for someone else, just as the man at table five had done for me.

FIGURES AMID THE FLAMES

by Debra Faust

I was putting the final load of clothes in the dryer at about 10:30 that overcast May night last year. When you have four kids at home you do a lot of wash. I was beat, and I figured I'd leave the folding until morning. I flipped the door shut and the dryer started with a determined rumble.

The laundry room was on the first floor of our old house, just off the living room, where my husband, Bob, sat watching television. I gave him a pat on the shoulder as I passed through. "Goin' up," I said as he squeezed my hand.

I made my way up the sturdy old staircase to the master bedroom, recently created by knocking down the wall between two smaller rooms. It was in the middle of a paint job. The mattress lay on the floor and much of the furniture lined the hallway. But that night I didn't mind. I just wanted to crawl into bed—wherever it was.

Alicia, 14, said good night and headed down the hall to the room she shared with her sister, Wendi, 12. The boys—Sean, 4, and Dale, 10—shared the other bedroom. I had every intention of grabbing my Bible from the stack of books beside my bed, but I fell asleep almost instantly to the drone of the TV coming up through the floor. I must not have been sleeping long because Bob's voice still came from downstairs when I awoke to the shock of him yelling, "Deb, the house is on fire!"

I jumped up, alert but a little disoriented. I stepped into the dark, cluttered hallway to be met by the overpowering stench of burning wood and insulation. "I can't use the phone!" Bob shouted up to me, his voice seeming to rise on a cloud of thick, billowing smoke. "I'll run next door!"

"Hurry!" I called back. "I'll get the kids."

I rushed to the boys' room. "Fire!" I shouted. "Get up! Fire!" I grabbed little Sean, but Dale slept soundly on the top bunk. I shook him. "Dale, get up! Fire!"

Then I shouted to the girls. Acrid smoke tumbled up the stairs, filling the hallway. My eyes stung and my chest burned. I stumbled toward my daughters' room. Everything was happening so quickly in a chaos of fear and confusion. I still had Sean in my arms. "Everybody out!" I screamed, but the words seemed to bounce back in my face in the engulfing smoke.

I met Alicia coming out of her room. She was dazed and coughing. I took her by the shoulders. "Get Wendi," I told her.

A horrible panic came over me. Blinded and short-winded, I went back to see if Dale was up. I could barely get enough air to shout. I bumped into Alicia again and asked about Wendi, but all she could do was gag. *Dale and Wendi must have got out.* Alicia, Sean and I felt our way to the bottom of the staircase, cringing from the heat and flames shooting out from the direction of the laundry room. Then we burst through the smoke and out onto the lawn.

I opened my eyes and gulped the sweet night air, pulling Sean and Alicia close. A sprinkling rain began to fall and it felt good on my skin. Bob ran up to us, eyes wide and searching. "Where's Dale?" he asked. "Where's Wendi?" I began screaming their names and looking all around me. Bob ran toward the house.

They're still inside. My babies are still inside!

"Mom," Alicia said, "I'm going in to find them."

"You can't go back in," I said, catching my breath and handing her a crying Sean. "I'll go."

I dashed up to the front door, where Bob was being driven back by the heat and smoke. He grabbed me. "I couldn't get farther than the landing, even on all fours," he gasped. "It's no use. The fire trucks will be here in a minute."

I fell to my knees sobbing, feeling utterly helpless. *Please, God, help them,* I screamed inside my heart. *Help them!* Bob and I began to yell, telling Wendi and Dale to follow our voices. My throat burned from the smoke but I kept yelling, my voice hoarse and cracked. Flames danced through the living room off to my left. I heard glass shattering and a roar like a giant blowtorch. The air itself seemed about to burst into flames. Directly in front of me I could make out the first few steps of the old stairway before it disappeared into an undulating cloud of smoke, tongues of flames lapping its sides. Where were my children?

Then, in that thick haze, two figures appeared on the stairs. They seemed unaffected in any way by the raging blaze. Such calmness glowed about them that I stopped crying. *Thank you, Lord,* I prayed, standing up. *Thank you.* A complete serenity overtook me. Time slowed, stilled.

All at once the figures were gone. One small hand pushed through the smoke. Dale! His daddy grabbed him, sweeping him into his arms. *Where is Wendi?* Then her hand emerged. I pulled her out and we fell back to the lawn, crying.

The six of us huddled together as if we would never let go, watching as our house went up in flames. Forty minutes earlier I had fallen fast asleep in my bed. Now my family and I were homeless, standing in the rain in our nightclothes. When the fire trucks pulled up, we retreated to our neighbor's front porch.

The old bricks in our house held in the tremendous heat, almost like a kiln, and the fire grew quickly, consuming almost everything. One fireman who tried to get in with a hose had his face shield melted. The firefighters said it was one of the hottest fires they had ever encountered. The investigation pointed to the dryer. Apparently, highly combustible lint had clogged the faulty exhaust hose. There wasn't much the firefighters could do to save our home once the blaze began.

Neighbors came to our rescue with jogging outfits to wear until we could buy clothes. People donated food and kept us in their prayers. We spent that first night with our pastor, then a week with friends. After another week in a motel, with the help of the American Red Cross and our church family, we were able to find an apartment. Clothing poured in, especially for the little guy, Sean. The school went into high gear to replace Wendi's and Dale's instruments so they could play in a band concert that first week. We always knew we lived in a wonderful community, but we found out just how wonderful our people could be. Mighty God reached out to us through the helping hands of neighbors and friends—angels each and every one.

There are earthly angels and there are heavenly angels. The two magnificent figures that appeared on the fiery staircase that night were sent by God to save my children, who miraculously escaped the flames unharmed and safe.

When Wendi told me, "Mom, someone pulled me out," we assumed she meant Dale. "No, Mom," he said, "I didn't even know she was there." We're convinced Wendi felt the hand of an angel!

Almost immediately we began building a new home on the same site. We moved in just in time for the holidays last year. Our Christmas tree had handmade decorations from family and friends. How thankful those holidays were! A house can always be rebuilt. God looks after families first—with angels at the ready.

A Brief Encounter

by John M. Segal

One summer, I took my son Jason to Chicago. As we got into the cab at Midway Airport, the driver started telling us how lousy his life was. "My wife is crazy," he said. "She's pregnant, and I want to have the child, but she doesn't. She drinks. She threw me out of the house. I don't know what to do."

We pulled up in front of the hotel, and I was thinking, *Lord, what do you want me to do?* So I asked him if he believed in God. He said "Yes" enthusiastically. I said, "Then I want you to pray for your wife. Pray with all your heart that she will be blessed." After some complaint, he agreed. Then I opened my briefcase and handed him a copy of Norman Vincent's Peale's *The Power of Positive Thinking.* He looked at it and said, "I'm a Muslim."

"Read it anyway; you'll like it," I told him.

Jason and I went to the hotel's registration desk, where we waited in line. When we finally got our key, I noticed that my briefcase was missing. All our tickets and travelers checks were in it. I ran to the entrance, knowing there was no chance a Chicago cabby would still be there after 20 minutes. But, there he was, a Muslim cab driver, still sitting at the curb absorbed in *The Power of Positive Thinking.*

Stranger with a Flask

by Paul DeLisle

The blizzard had raged all day, blanketing the farm with snow and obliterating the roads. Drifts were piled as high as the house. Inside, as night fell, a 10-year-old boy lay in bed, gasping for air. His lungs were weak, the result of having been born prematurely. On that February night in 1933 he had bronchitis and his throat was clogged with phlegm. There was no phone to call a doctor, but even if there had been, none could have made it in this weather. Besides, doctors had given up on the boy's health years ago.

His mother never gave up, though. Ali would say, "Son, I'm not afraid of you dyin'. I know you'd be safe and happy in heaven. But if it's God's will you live, I'm going to help you all I can."

The boy had suffered severe colds before and Ali's home remedies always pulled him through. But this time none of her treatments made a difference. His skin had turned a deathly gray-blue. She placed mustard plasters on his chest and under his back. She applied more Vicks to his forehead, smoothing his blond curls. As she listened to the storm howling around their farmhouse and the worsening wheeze in her son's chest, her lips moved in silent prayer. Her husband was nursing his arthritis in the next room. The closest neighbor lived a quarter-mile away. "What more can I do, Lord?" she asked.

A loud knocking startled her, and she sat quickly upright in her rocker next to the boy's bed. *Who can be out on a night like this?* Ali wondered as she hurried to the kitchen door. A tall man stood on the porch, his coat collar turned up around his face and his hat pulled tightly over his head. In the Depression it wasn't unusual for people down on their luck to stop by and ask for work in exchange for food or a warm place to sleep. "Come in," Ali said. "Make yourself at home." She gestured to the coffeepot and teakettle warming on the stove. "My little boy is sick," Ali said. "I need to get back to him." But the stranger called after her, "Wait!"

He pointed to a mug on the table. "Fill it half full of hot water," he said. Ali, worn out and desperate, snatched up the mug and obediently sloshed water from the kettle into it. "Bring it here," he told her. He pulled a flask from his coat and filled the mug with what looked and smelled like whiskey. "Pour this down your son's throat," he said. "Get it all into him."

Ali raced to her boy's room, sat him up and began pouring the near-scalding mixture into his mouth. His face turned fiery red and his eyes opened wide. He grabbed her arm but she tilted his head back and emptied the mug down his throat. The boy gagged, choking and spitting, unable to breathe. Then the hot liquid began to do its work, breaking up the phlegm. Ali held him close to her until he had rid himself of it all. Finally, completely spent, the boy lay down, breathing easily. His skin returned to a healthy pink. "I have to go thank that man," Ali said.

But the kitchen was empty. She called to her husband, "Ed, did you see the man leave?" The boy's dad appeared in the doorway, moving stiffly. "I never saw him at all," he said. "Maybe he's gone out to sleep in the barn." Ed sat down, painfully pulling on his boots. "I'll go tell him to come back in." But Ed found no one in the barn.

The boy listened to his parents in the kitchen as they talked about the stranger.

"I didn't hear Shep bark, did you, Ali?" Ed asked.

"That's why the knock startled me so," said Ali.

The boy grinned. Their dog went nuts even when a car passed.

"And something else," Ali said thoughtfully. "There's no sign he was here. No melted snow, no wet rugs, no used mug. Ed, when you went out to look for him, the cold air hit me with a blast! I didn't feel any cold air when I let him in."

That winter night was 63 years ago on my family's farm in Alverno, Michigan. I was the boy. Some who have heard this story say they knew of the hot whiskey remedy, and were surprised my mother didn't think of it. But Ma was dead set against alcohol. She never allowed it in the house, not before and not after that visit. She always welcomed strangers in need, though. That extraordinary night God sent her one who took care of her needs instead, and saved my life.

Our Mysterious Man in Bulgaria

by Laura S. Curran

Stephen and I held hands as the plane took off from Frankfurt, Germany, and headed east. We had left the world we knew far behind that January day in 1992. My husband and I had boarded this antiquated Russian-made aircraft en route to Sofia, Bulgaria, where we planned to adopt 13-month-old twin girls. Although we knew them only from photographs, we had already grown to love them. Now, after four long months, we were close to fulfilling our dream.

Fog shrouded Sofia as we approached the city. The pilot announced we would land in the small town of Plovdiv instead, 130 kilometers from Sofia, far from the hotel where representatives of the adoption agency were expecting us. Stephen saw the flash of worry cross my face and squeezed my arm.

The chaotic Plovdiv airport did nothing to ease my anxiety. Hundreds of cigarette-puffing Bulgarians pushed their way toward two overworked customs agents. We struggled to find a place in line. Everything seemed to be going against us: the language, the locale—and our luggage. Along with a small suitcase, we were carrying 11 large duffel bags full of medical supplies donated for the other children at the orphanage. I looked around frantically, praying for some kind of help.

And there he was. He would have stood out anywhere, this handsome man, well dressed and carrying an expensive briefcase. He motioned to us. "This is your place in line," he said in perfect English. "Here, in front of me." We happily complied.

We had been told by the U.S. Embassy that visas weren't necessary to enter Bulgaria, but the customs agent demanded to see them. Bulgaria's government was in transition; the laws sometimes changed overnight. We showed the agent our passports, and he shook his head. Had we come this close only to have to return without our girls?

Then the well-dressed gentleman stepped forward and spoke a few words in Bulgarian. The agent immediately passed us through. Dragging our duffel bags to the Sofia bus, I glanced back at the man whose words had held such power.

After a two-hour ride we arrived in Sofia. The other passengers dispersed, leaving only us and our bags. A driver approached us. "Taxi?" he asked, quoting an exorbitant fee. What if he tried to charge even more, or steal our valuable cargo? I looked at Stephen. We were both thinking of the twins. *What choice do we have but to get in the taxi?*

Suddenly the man who had assisted us in Plovdiv was at our side, although he had not been with us on the bus. He proceeded to negotiate an honest fare from a couple of taxi drivers. We divided the baggage, and Stephen rode in one cab, our guide and I in the other.

"What do you do in Bulgaria?" I finally asked. "I work with the government," he said. "My name is Christos."

At the hotel our newfound friend wished us well and then walked off into the foggy night. The trials of our trip were over. A few days later we were home with our twins, thanks to our mysterious man in Bulgaria.

The Coin Exchange

by Rhoda Blecker

Proclaim liberty throughout all the land unto all the inhabitants thereof....
— Leviticus 25:10

On a ferry between Dover and Holland in the early 1970s, I found myself sitting across from a woman from Romania. Her name was Daniela; she'd come to England for dental work and was now on her way home. She told me the Romanian government was holding her ten-year-old daughter as hostage against her return from the West. I was sympathetic, if not entirely able to understand her predicament.

As we neared our landing point, Daniela fished out a leu from her purse, the basic Romanian coin, and gave it to me. It had a tractor on it. I scrabbled around in my purse and found a quarter, handing it to her in return. She studied it for a moment, then looked up at me with tears in her eyes, and said, "'Liberty.' You even put it on the money."

I was suddenly prouder than I had been in years to be an American. I've never forgotten that pride. It was a gift of awareness, of recognition that God did shed His grace on my nation, and that I was very fortunate to be part of it.

Thank You, God, for a country that stands for liberty and justice for all. May I do my part today to uphold Your blessing.

Desert Rescue

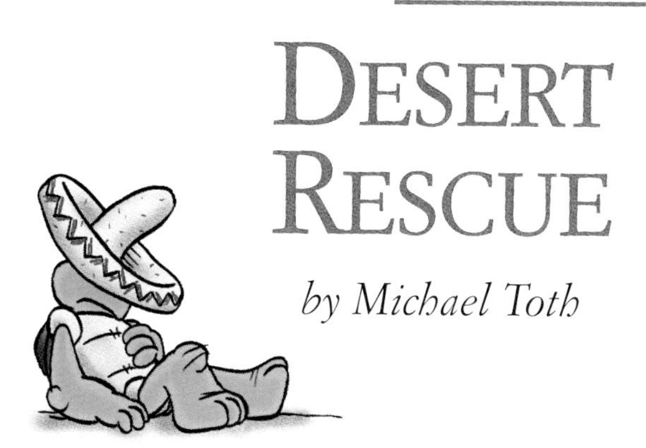

by Michael Toth

"Why won't anyone stop to help us?" Mom asked as a car whizzed past, ignoring my sister's frantic waves.

It was almost fifty miles through the desert to the next town, and I knew there was no way the three of us could walk that. And Mom didn't have a clue as to what was wrong with our car.

"Let's get in out of the sun," Mom said. We all climbed back into the car. "We'd better pray," she said.

I didn't know exactly what to pray for. An angel with a tow truck? Still, we all bowed our heads and asked God to help.

After a while, we saw a blue Toyota truck coming down the road. He pulled right up to us, as if he knew we'd be there. An older couple got out. "We were on another highway," the lady said, "and we heard in our prayers that someone needed our help."

That seemed a little weird to me. But the man was a mechanic and found out the problem right away. "Your battery's dead. I'll take it and get it recharged."

Then the lady handed us a bag of sandwiches and assured us that they'd be back.

So we ate and waited. Sure enough, a few hours later they came back with a charged-up battery.

The old lady put her hands on Mom's cheeks and said, "You'll be all right, Cheryl." Then she turned to me and my sister. "Michael and Janet," she said, "be good to your mommy. See that she gets home safely to Indiana."

Then, they were gone. Suddenly, it hit us. That lady had called us by name—all of us. And she knew that we were going to Indiana. *But we'd never told them any of that stuff!*

Surprisingly, it didn't seem all that weird to me. After all, the One who told them where we were had heard our prayers—and knew our names.

We not only live among men,
but there are airy hosts,
blessed spectators, sympathetic
lookers-on, that see and know
and appreciate our thoughts
and feelings and acts.

—Henry Ward Beecher

4 Back Home

But trailing clouds of glory
do we come from God,
who is our home.

— William Wordsworth

Blossoming of the Cross

by Jeanne Hill

It was the day before Easter and I couldn't stop fretting. My husband, Louis, and I were on a plane to Texas, about to spend a week with our daughter, Dawn, and her 12-year-old son, Harrison. A single parent, Dawn had moved from San Francisco six months before, to take a teaching job in Waco, and had gone farm hunting until she finally found a place she could buy with her nest egg. When I quizzed her on the phone, she admitted her dream house was 80 years old, out in the country on 10 acres, and had no central heating or air-conditioning.

"Considering how little she paid for it, it's got to be dilapidated," I told my husband. "It's so impractical. She's let herself get carried away by romantic notions about life in the country."

I tried to keep my doubts from showing when Dawn and Harrison picked us up at the airport. But my worst fears were realized when I caught sight of her green-and-white house. Ripped screens lay in the weeds where they had fallen out of windows, and the front steps were caved in.

Inside were more problems. The dishwasher hiccuped. The back door had a broken handle so the door wouldn't stay closed unless it was locked. Dawn's apartment furniture was so dwarfed in the high-ceilinged rooms that the place had the look of a barn. And in a field in the back I saw a bull! Dawn didn't know a thing about livestock. What on earth was she thinking?

That night Louis gave my shoulder a reassuring pat. "It will be all right, Honey," he said. "These things can be fixed."

"By whom?" I wanted to shout. Dawn and Harrison clearly didn't know what they were doing.

I hardly slept, cataloging everything that was wrong with my daughter's new home and the move she'd made. I went over how I would advise Dawn the next morning about all the changes I thought necessary. First off, she'd have to hire a carpenter to repair everything, then she'd have to rearrange her furniture. And of course she would have to get rid of that bull; she certainly didn't know how to care for it. Thank goodness I had arrived to straighten things out.

When daylight finally arrived I threw on a robe and ran to talk to my daughter. But she and Harrison were nowhere in the house. I followed the barking of their dogs to the meadow adjoining the backyard. There in the golden morning light my daughter and grandson stood. . . . picking flowers!

Dawn turned and spotted me. "Hi, Mom. You're in for a special Easter." She held up the flowers. "We're going to blossom the cross."

Easter morning! I had been so engrossed with my fretting that for a moment I had almost forgotten. "Dawn, we need to talk," I said. But then Louis appeared and the rush was on to get ready for church. Okay, I would talk to her later. . . .

We pulled up to the church and I saw others getting out of their cars carrying baskets of flowers. Dawn and Harrison carried their flowers up the aisle to a polished oak table directly in front of the pulpit. By the time the service started the table was overflowing with garden flowers—red and pink roses, blue snapdragons, white lilies and yellow jonquils—and wildflowers of vivid blue, gold and scarlet. The fragrances filled the sanctuary.

In stark contrast to the vibrant flowers stood a cross, about eight feet high, of ugly rough beams covered by a layer of chicken wire. At the end of the service the minister rose. "In the days preceding this glorious morning," he said, "our focus has been on the cruelty and violence of the cross itself. But Christ turned its ugliness into beauty.

Now we'll do the same by blossoming the cross this Easter Sunday."

As the organ music swelled, the congregation formed two lines, one on each side of the table, facing the altar. Each man, woman and child passed the table and chose a few flowers, then stepped up to weave the blossoms into the wire mesh covering the cross. The men filled the top, the women adorned the crossbar, and the children added blooms from the floor to as high as they could reach.

When my turn came I picked up some iris and a spray of bluebonnets. As I leaned in to fasten the fragrant blossoms onto the cross, I saw Dawn's face opposite me as she did the same. I looked down toward where Harrison bent, proudly affixing the flowers he had chosen. Both their expressions were filled with excitement and wonder as they participated in this symbolic ritual of new life. And then it struck me. Dawn and Harrison were blossoming in a whole new life too. And now I had to blossom—and allow them to blossom—by giving up my desire to rush in and fix things.

The entire structure was covered. We stepped back from the now beautiful, sweet-smelling cross to hold hands as a family, and as a part of the congregation.

As we drove back to Dawn's house I looked around at the beautiful meadows and wooded hills. "We've got a creek," Harrison told me excitedly. "And a spring." Dawn and Harrison showed me the pecan tree just outside Harrison's bedroom window "where our owl family lives," and the berm by the creek "where our armadillo stays." As we entered the house I marveled at all the beauty my critical eyes had missed—lovely old wood floors and a stately fieldstone fireplace.

Once I got used to those high ceilings the furniture didn't look so sparse after all. Later, when we got the screens up we realized the windows channeled refreshing cross breezes. And later that week, as we all hammered away fixing the front-porch steps, the 500-pound bull wandered over, wrapped his tongue around Dawn's shirt tail and started sucking on it. Dawn put down the hammer and rubbed the animal's thick neck. "Come on, Norman, let's get your dinner," she said, leading him away as though she had been cow wrangling all her life.

What on earth was Dawn thinking? Why, she'd been thinking of having her own life. And I was now thinking of tending to mine—and I'd start by suggesting we blossom the cross at our own church back home next year.

THAT DREADED TERM PAPER

by Charlene Terrell

Everyone in my accounting class knew it was inevitable, but when our professor at Georgia State University, Dr. Norman Dressel, crisply outlined the requirements of the lengthy term paper, he sounded especially forbidding. As he regarded us with his piercing eyes, his summation said it all: "Of course, content *is* important, but so is *proper* form and *precise* bibliography and annotation." The dread in the classroom seemed to weight the air.

After the bell, as my classmates filed out mumbling darkly, I recalled another classroom, that of Mrs. Ado Coots, the terror of Forsyth County High. If exacting attention to the most infinitesimal detail had a hall of fame, Mrs. Ado Coots would be the first person inducted. I could still picture her neat script in the margins of my English papers, carefully enumerating each of my grammatical shortcomings in bright blue ink.

"One of these days," Mrs. Coots was fond of saying, "you students will find that what you're learning here will be useful." Few of us believed her, but that didn't discourage Mrs. Coots from her relentless drilling in the basics of English composition. She was unwavering in her determination that we master the intricacies of an annotated term paper with a proper bibliography. At the slightest protest, Mrs. Coots's dark eyes flashed. "You will find that the real world is *far* more demanding than my term papers, but meanwhile they can help prepare you for it!"

I smiled at the memory. Nothing had been more difficult than one of her term papers, not even the prospect of one of Professor Dressel's. Not that I wasn't quaking in my boots: He was a notoriously hard grader, seeming to take particular delight in giving Cs to A students. The next day I threw myself into the paper, working harder on it than any project I could remember.

When he handed back our papers, groans from the disappointed made Professor Dressel's classroom sound like a hospital ward. He tossed my paper on my desk without comment. I shut my eyes tightly, steeling myself for the blow. When I cracked them open, an A+ leaped off the page. In disbelief I bent over for a closer look. Professor Dressel had written a terse note just below the grade: "See me after class."

Nervously I approached his desk as the others grumbled out. "Young lady," he said, "your term paper is among the finest I have ever seen produced by a junior accounting student. Do you know what this tells me?"

I shook my head.

"It tells me that somewhere along the line you had a remarkable English teacher. If he or she is still alive, you should go to that teacher and express your gratitude. Good night."

He snapped his textbook closed, abruptly stood and strode out.

My mouth gaped. In my heart I knew Professor Dressel was right; I owed a good measure of my A+ to Mrs. Coots. I knew I should thank her, but the memory of her no-nonsense, crisp classroom demeanor still intimidated me.

On the evening I finally forced myself up to the front door of her modest house, I was trembling. But the woman who answered the door was far different from the Mrs. Coots I remembered in the classroom. She was in a bathrobe—pale and frowning. "May I come in?" I blurted.

She coughed and reluctantly beckoned me in. "I've been sick all fall," she said in a reedy voice. "I'm just now getting over pneumonia."

Mrs. Coots half collapsed in a chair and regarded me tiredly. I sat on the edge of the chair nearest her. I thrust my term paper into her hands. She glanced at it, then looked back at me quizzically.

"My accounting professor knew someone like you was responsible for my paper—and—uh—" I stammered, "I just wanted to thank you. I really appreciate all you did for me."

Mrs. Coots began to cry. "You're the first person ever to thank me," she sobbed. "This has been such a hard year, but your visit has done me more good than all the medicine I've taken. God bless you!" She got up, raised me gently out of my chair, threw her arms around me and hugged me hard. Then we *both* shed some tears. "I'm so glad you stopped by," she said.

"So am I!" I replied.

Mrs. Coots was a candidate for a hall of fame all right, but of a higher order than I originally thought. Her appointment would be for teachers who give abundantly so their students might prosper. Encircled in her loving hug, I knew some of the bread that Mrs. Coots had so tirelessly cast upon the waters had now been found, after many days.*

Never again have I been reluctant to express gratitude.

* Ecclesiastes 11:1, paraphrased

A Boy's Lesson in Things Eternal

by Marion F. Ash

I was a teenager during the depression years. Those were dark times for a farm boy, especially one like me who hadn't yet learned to trust in a Heavenly Father. I suppose, as my mother told me often enough, I needed numerous lessons in faith, and I believe one of the most remembered was the day a letter came to our mailbox for old Mrs. Totten who lived down the road a mile from us.

My mother looked at the letter. "It's from her daughter Bertha. Marion, you better take it to her."

"But, Mom . . . . "

"You better. Something tells me we ought to get the letter to Mrs. Totten."

Mother was everlastingly sending me to the old lady's house for one reason or another because she had certain feelings that things ought to be done. My mother's feelings puzzled me; in fact, she believed in things I could not see or feel or touch or taste. My mother called these things eternal. She seemed as sure of these as she did the little house she scrubbed and cleaned and made nice for us to live in.

And whenever my mother began telling about the eternal things, she always mentioned how God works in mysterious ways His wonders to perform. Once I asked her what some of the mysterious things were and she told me about the time my little sister was sick and they couldn't get the doctor because he was out of town. And then that afternoon he passed our house on his way home, and how he had to stop to get some water for his car's radiator. Before leaving, the doctor examined my little sister, and left some medicine for my mother to give her every hour on the hour.

Once she looked at me and said, "Someday you'll get the feelings, too. Then maybe you'll understand what I'm talking about."

I wondered what the feeling was she had about getting this letter to old Mrs. Totten. She didn't say; she only went on talking as if to herself about this being the first springtime that Mrs. Totten had ever faced without Mr. Totten.

I took the letter and went.

Mrs. Totten was a sweet old lady. When I got there, she was standing under her ancient apple tree. "It's going to put out again," she remarked as I approached. Then she looked at me and said, "What a faithful Heavenly Father we have. He promised, 'As long as the earth endures, seedtime and harvest, cold and heat, summer and winter, day and night will never cease'" (Genesis 8:22). Old Mrs. Totten could quote Scripture as well as my mother, and I tried to change the subject by saying, "Here's a letter that came to our mailbox for you." She took it and went back to the porch and sat down.

She took the corner of her apron and wiped her spectacles. Then she picked up the envelope from her lap and looked at it. "Why it's from Bertha!" she exclaimed. "It's been so long since she's written."

I watched a frown come to her face as she read the letter. When she had finished, she said, "Bertha says I'm getting too old to stay by myself. She wants me to come and live with her."

She looked toward the orchard, the barn and the garden. To me, the place looked still and empty. I remembered folks talking about how Mrs. Totten had to sell the team of horses and other things to pay the expenses of Mr. Totten's long illness and death.

"Yes," she finally said, "springtime has come. That apple tree is going to bloom again. It's older than I am. My pa set it out before I was born. We grew up together. If I leave, it can't pick up and go with me."

For a moment, she was silent. Then she turned and looked at me. "Marion, would you mind to answer the letter to Bertha? I shake so. Then you can take it back and mail it."

"Be glad to," I answered, a little curious as to what she was going to tell Bertha.

I could not understand what there was about the old place for her to cling to. The roof was mossy and falling in. The barn was leaning. The fences were all down, and the gate had settled into the earth and stood eternally open. But it did seem a sort of standing invitation to come in.

Inside, she found paper, a pencil, an envelope and postage from a drawer of a little corner table.

"Just tell Bertha," old Mrs. Totten began, "that I got along good through the winter. Tell her the Lord has been good to me. Tell her it's springtime again, that the old apple tree is fixing to bloom. Tell her not to worry herself about the plowing. Of course, I'm not able to plow, and have no team of horses either, but tell her there were many things in my seventy years that the Lord has done for me. Just tell her I'm not aiming to leave here. Tell her to come as soon as she can to see me."

I had to write furiously to get it all down.

When I saw she didn't have anymore to say, I grabbed my hat and ran home so I could tell my mother what old Mrs. Totten had me write.

"She even wrote to Bertha that the Lord would help her get her garden plowed," I told mother.

Mom looked at me, I thought quite sternly, then said, "Mrs. Totten has faith. She believes the Scripture verse that says: 'Now faith is being sure of what we hope for and certain of what we do not see' (Hebrews 11:1). The Lord will help people like her, people who believe in things eternal."

"But how?" I asked.

"The Lord works in mysterious ways," Mom said.

"But He never helped Pa and me plow."

"Oh, yes, He did," explained my mother. "He gave your father and you good health and strong arms and hands," Mom pointed out. Then she went on how the Lord didn't have to help people who could do for themselves, and how it was things a person couldn't do that the Lord helped him do.

But still I could not understand such things. I wondered if I would ever know as much about eternal things as my mother.

I did not begin to get an inkling of the things of which my mother and old Mrs. Totten spoke until the following morning at the breakfast table.

"Marion, as soon as you have eaten, I want you to harness the team of horses."

"Why?" I asked, trying to shake the sleep from my eyes. I couldn't recall Pa saying anything about doing any plowing today.

"I want you to take the plow and harrow and get Mrs. Totten's garden ready for her to plant."

"What!" I exclaimed. "But that'll take all day, and she can't pay anything."

"I'll fix you a sack lunch," my mother said, "and you will get paid."

I asked her who was going to pay and how much, and she said the best kind of pay for some kinds of work was not money. Mother said that I would never regret it.

It didn't make much sense to me that day, but I harnessed the horses and let them drag an old sled, with the plow and harrow on it, down the road to Mrs. Totten's. And all the way, I kept wondering what feelings Mom had that prompted this project. Whatever her feelings were—this time, like most of the rest—they always caused me to do something extra. Suddenly, I was thinking that the Lord sure does work in mysterious ways His wonders to perform.

I remember Mrs. Totten went out to the garden gate when she heard and saw me, and I can see her plain to this day, her face set in a frame of silvered hair, her hand shading her eyes from the sun.

I explained that my mother had sent me and she started to say something but didn't finish on account of a break in her voice and she started toward the house. After I started plowing, I saw her coming with a big old rusty bucket of seed potatoes.

The rich brown earth seemed hungry for seed, and from the fields came scents and sounds of spring and a call for all things to live again.

Old Mrs. Totten got a hoe and started planting potatoes. Just watching her and feeling the rich earth rolling around my ankles made me think of things. I thought of the letter I had written for her, and the things she had said. And I, too, began to have feelings about things eternal and in the heavens.

Something inside of me told me I was answering the letter I had written for the old lady. I thought how true the Scripture was for the old lady that believed: "According to your faith will it be done you" (Matthew 9:29).

That afternoon, I saw old Mrs. Totten leaning on the garden gate, and I knew she was waiting for me to finish. I thought she looked so good, as if she were a part of the earth herself, and just back of her were the pink blossoms of the peach tree.

When I had finished, I turned the horses through the gate toward the road. I nearly got past her, but then she caught hold of my arm.

"Tell your ma," she said ever so softly, "there's an eternal home waiting for her up in the sky."

I guess she put it simple like that so a boy like me could understand, and I did. As the horses dragged the sled up the road, a lot of things that had been dim and far off now were plain and close.

When I got to the barn, my mother was waiting for me, for that was like her after she had sent me off on an errand like this. I could tell she was really anxious to know how things had gone, and if the old lady was happy because I had helped her get her garden ready for planting.

"What did Mrs. Totten say?" Mom asked.

"Oh, she was real glad. She said to tell you that there's an eternal home in heaven waiting for you."

My mother looked far off again and she thought it over for a few minutes.

"Are you glad you plowed her garden?" she finally asked.

"Yes, Mom. I feel kind of good about it now."

And through the years, I have. For that was a day long ago, and my mother and old Mrs. Totten are gone now. Sometimes I feel kind of lonely, and I walk down past Mrs. Totten's old place. I do this mostly in the spring.

I stand there in the road and look to where the house once stood. The ancient apple tree is gone and so are the other fruit trees. But I remember.

I stand still and listen and feel. I hear the meadowlarks in a nearby field, and I feel the soft spring breeze blowing across my face.

I glance up in the clear blue of a springtime sky, and I know—I know two mothers live in an eternal home up there.

Then my heart wells with faith and I can almost shout with the Apostle Paul:

"No eyes have seen, no ears have heard, no mind has conceived what God has prepared for those who love Him" (I Corinthians 2:9).

The Town That Helped the Cows Come Home

by Alvin Kleman

I'm a lifelong farmer, like my father before me and three of the seven children my wife Dorothy and I raised on our spread outside Nazareth, Texas, the land my granddaddy farmed. Like most farmers, I take pride in self-sufficiency and independence. A couple of years ago, though, a neighbor named Ralph Albracht and a lot of other good people taught me not to put too much pride in those things.

Had anyone asked, I would have said that the worst thing that could happen to a dairy farmer like me was for his barn to burn down. My granddaddy built our barn in 1947. When Dorothy and I took over the farm, we renovated the old wooden structure into a dairy barn, hand-digging a long trench so the cows stood on one level with the milkers below them. We scrimped and saved through the years to put in electrical lines and add modern milking machines. By 1984 we had branched out into raising beef cattle and growing our own feed.

Three of my boys work with me. Dwayne is in charge of the farming, Joe handles the beef cattle and Mark runs the dairy. But from August to October all four of us have to work dawn to dusk to bring in the silage harvest. On the evening of October 4, 1994, I turned in tired but grateful. After two years of drought, our first good harvest was in the silos, ripe and dry. Relieved, I fell into a deep sleep.

It was before dawn when Joe burst into our bedroom shouting, "Dad! Dad, get up! The barn is on fire!"

I've never come awake so fast in my life. I threw on my old jeans and flannel shirt. Joe grabbed the phone but the line was dead. "I'm going over to Dwayne's to call the fire department," he yelled, and was gone.

When Dorothy and I raced outside, the heat was like a punch in the face. The barn was ablaze from one end to the other. Flames shot straight into the sky like a gigantic blowtorch. I was glad the cows were all outside in their pens.

Dorothy wept softly as I pulled her close, fighting a losing battle against my own tears. "There goes our whole life," I said.

"What do we do now, Alvin?" Dorothy asked.

I shook my head and didn't speak. It was all gone.

By then the volunteer fire departments of Nazareth and nearby Dimmitt had arrived, and the narrow road leading to our place was choked with vehicles. Neighbors arrived too, not even asking how to help. They just pitched in. Someone got some cinnamon rolls started in the kitchen and by six o'clock, as the flames died out, there was enough food to feed our family and all the volunteers.

Dorothy and I walked through drifts of smoke, surveying the damage. The barn had burned to its foundation. As neighbors joined the firefighters in clearing away the charred debris, I couldn't imagine starting over. Dorothy and I were in our sixties. *Lord, what do we do now?* I wondered.

Gradually I became aware of a sound rising in the background. It was our dairy herd, bawling pitifully. Trotting to the pens, I looked into their huge, pleading eyes. I could see milk already dripping from their swollen udders. We had 300 head and somehow we had to get them milked.

That's when Ralph Albracht, whose dairy farm was three miles down the road, walked up. My sons were behind him. "Alvin," he said calmly, "I've talked it over with your boys and they agree with me. You bring those cows over to my place and we'll milk 'em there."

"I can't do that, Ralph," I replied. That was too much of a burden to place on any farmer, and I had never been a burden to a neighbor. "I can't ask that of you."

Ralph pushed his hat back on his head. "You're not asking, Alvin. I'm offerin'."

Joe stepped forward. "Dad," he pleaded, "listen to that herd. At least let's take 'em over for milkin' now. Then we'll decide what to do."

I still couldn't accept it. I had never had to ask anyone for help.

By now, Dorothy had joined us. "Alvin," she said, "Ralph and the boys are right. This is what we need to do." Finally, reluctantly, I agreed.

Ralph smiled and slapped me on the back. "I appreciate you lettin' me help, Alvin."

A couple of fellows stepped up and proposed loading the animals onto their 18-wheel rigs, but I figured it would be easier on the cows if we herded them the old cowboy way the three miles to the Albrachts'. Everyone agreed and went off to saddle up horses. By 9:00 A.M. a dozen riders started the first drive of 150 cows down the dirt road in back of our farm. Dorothy and I went ahead in our pickup to hold traffic while the herd passed. "I still feel pretty peculiar about the whole situation," I confessed. "I don't like imposing."

"Alvin," she said, "you know you'd do the same for Ralph." She was right. I guess it's easier sometimes to give help than to ask for it.

When we got the first group of cows to Ralph's spread about 11 o'clock, I could hardly believe my eyes. A separate area had already been fenced off. Feeders were in place and clean, cool water brimmed in the troughs. Neighbors and townsfolk I had seen cleaning the debris from our charred barn now began coaxing the cows into Ralph's barn.

I felt a rush of gratitude. *Lord, how will I ever repay these good folks?* I was overwhelmed.

Ralph sauntered up. "You know, Alvin," he said, "you might as well leave these cows here until you rebuild. You can milk your herd in the mornings when I'm finished doing mine."

That would mean Ralph running his milking machines 18 hours a day . . . indefinitely.

"That would be too much to ask, Ralph."

Ralph regarded me evenly. It was just the two of us, leaning on an old fence. "Maybe I'm gettin' old, Alvin," he said quietly, "but lately I've been thinking about how blessed I've been. I reckon I've always been too busy building up this dairy to lend a hand where I might have. Today when I saw your barn go up, it seemed like God spoke to me: 'Okay, Ralph, here's your chance to help someone.' I don't want to force anything on you, but it would mean a lot if you let me help."

I swallowed the lump in my throat. I needed to do some thinking.

Over the next couple of days Dorothy, the boys and I looked at the situation every kind of way. In the end, for the sake of a farm that had been in our family for the better part of a century, I knew I had to rebuild. Quitting just wasn't an option.

We had a few tough months ahead of us. The boys and I were up at 4:00 A.M. for our first turn on the milkers. Then we worked our fields and the beef herd until sundown, when we went back to the Albrachts' for our second milking shift. Our other four children returned—one from Korea—to pitch in. As my son John said, "This farm's been good to us, Dad. It's time we gave something back."

The hardworking construction crew put up a new barn in 74 days. On the seventy-fifth day, December 19, the whole town of Nazareth turned out to help drive the cows back from Ralph Albracht's place. This time it was a celebration, like a Wild West party with people hootin' and hollerin' and whistlin', riding tall in the saddle and driving the cattle across the West Texas prairie as generations had before.

When the herd turned onto our property, Dorothy was waiting with huge steaming kettles of chili. After we finally got the last stragglers into their holding pens, I saw Ralph at the end of the chili line, patiently waiting his turn. I felt bad for having fought him so hard in the beginning. What I learned was that my need was an answer to his prayer. The Lord wants us to help one another out, which means that a stubborn old cuss like me has to push his pride aside from time to time.

I went over to Ralph and extended my hand. I looked from him to our new barn. At that moment I felt it was as if he and the whole town had stepped right out of the Bible to show me how to live—how to receive and in the future, God willing, how to give.

Seasons of Life

by Elizabeth Sherrill

I didn't think, as we stepped into the bleak little restaurant, that I would leave it carrying a gift from God.

It was February, a midweek night, and the forlorn café on the dusty outskirts of Brignoles, in southern France, was the only eating place open. It was just the sort of spot, my husband John and I reminded ourselves, where we had eaten all the time in our early days over here. *We were young*, I thought. *More adaptable.*

Our host, who was also the chef and the sole other diner, brought us a platter of gristly looking meat and with a cordial, "Bon appétit!" went back to his own meal.

"Remember how hungry we'd be after biking all day?" I said to John as he sawed valiantly at the meat. In our younger days we hadn't needed a car to travel around in. *We had a lot more energy then.*

Something else was different too—years ago we would have struck up a conversation with the friendly proprietor, maybe discovered a fascinating story. He was a small, stooped, bright-faced individual, dressed in the jacket of a blue suit and the pants of a brown one. It would be hard to talk about anything very complicated now; we had forgotten a lot of our French. *Your memory starts to go as you get older.*

Thinking back came naturally just then. This was 1997, an anniversary trip exactly 50 years after John and I met and married here in Europe. But if memories were welcome, comparisons were not. The contrast was too great between that young bride and the gray-haired woman who had looked back at me from the cracked glass in the restaurant washroom.

All day we had driven through a lifeless winter landscape, the freshness of spring long past. I remembered asking God as we traveled along roads lined with leafless poplars, "What is this season of life for? Just . . . looking back?"

"*Café*?" the little proprietor asked as he picked up our plates.

Soon we heard the hiss of steam, which meant a strong black espresso was brewing. Several minutes passed but no coffee appeared. At last the man emerged from his pocket-handkerchief of a kitchen, two small coffee cups in one hand and in the other a great sheaf of feathery leaves dotted with round yellow flowers.

"*Pour vous, madame*!" he said, presenting the spray to me with a Gallic flourish.

I took the astounding branch from his hand—lacy fernlike leaves and a hundred bright pom-poms, lighting the shabby room like so many miniature sunbursts.

"Why . . . where did these come from!" I marveled.

"From the garden." He gestured toward the back of the building.

Now? In February? "A greenhouse," John guessed.

"*Mais non*!" From his garden, our host insisted. He waved his hand again. "Out there."

"But," I protested, "nothing's blooming at this time of year!"

"Why yes, madame! Acacia blooms all through the year. Always it has flowers. Summer, winter—every season."

Acacia blooms in every season . . .

The proprietor drew a chair up to our table and suddenly we found ourselves talking like old friends. And in the morning in our hotel room basin, the acacia flowers had opened wider, so that it seemed impossible a single branch could hold so many blossoms. A brand-new day stretched ahead, with a few hundred new things I wanted to explore and do.

Not the same things I did 50 years ago. My memory wasn't as sharp, perhaps, my energy less. But today was today—with different insights, different adventures. A time for the flowering of the season at hand.

Trust and a Sense of Humor

by Brenda Wilbee

Two years ago, I went to Washington, D.C., to visit a friend, and I left my two teenagers home alone. Phillip was sixteen, Blake fourteen. *Would they be all right? Would they get into an accident? What if something terrible happened at school? Would the house burn down? What if they trashed the house?*

I returned home eight days later at three in the morning. The boys had left on a lamp, there was a welcome-home note on the counter, the house was in perfect order. When I opened the door to my bedroom, I laughed out loud.

There was a man in my bed! A pair of blue jeans had been carefully laid out, with dirty socks for feet. A T-shirt made up the chest. Rolled-up posters worked for arms, mittens served as hands, the head was a Dave Barry book, propped against my pillow. A baseball cap topped everything off. And stacked on the T-shirt? A pile of presents.

Nothing untoward had happened. My boys had even missed me and gone out of their way to welcome me home.

The Unexpected Grandson

by Norma Simpson

When you're my age life tends to settle down, without the surprises it once held. At 85, I had grown comfortable with my daily routine in a small lake community in southeast Texas called Toledo Bend. Getting the mail was often a highlight of my day. And that's where I was one summer afternoon a couple years ago—standing at the mailbox—when I opened a red-white-and-blue express-mail envelope and got the shock of my life.

"My name is Tony," the letter read. The writer went on to explain carefully, "I'm your grandson and I'd like to come to meet you." I turned the envelope over and checked the postmark. *All the way from the East Coast. A far piece to travel for a hoax,* I thought. Because it just couldn't be true. Could it?

I was thrown back in time, to 1955. My only child, Dorothy, single, in her mid 20s and living at home, had been crying for days. It just about killed me to see her brilliant blue eyes rimmed with red. Finally she said, "Mother, I'm pregnant."

"Who is the father?" I managed to ask. Dorothy told me. Later I found out he was married. She hadn't known.

Dorothy was a bright girl, who graduated from college with a degree in journalism. She had a good job. Her father had died when she was barely out of her teens. We were as close as two people could be. We loved board games and had a closetful, passing many an evening intent on our strategies. We liked bird-watching, though Dorothy was better at recognizing the rare ones than I was. We laughed like old friends. We were more than mother and daughter; we were a team. And we decided we would raise the baby the way we did most things: together.

Being an unwed mother carried a terrible stigma in our small town. Dorothy and I turned to the church for counseling. During many sessions with our pastor we discussed what the years had in store for my daughter. We learned of all the couples who were desperate to have a baby, but couldn't. Was it right to deprive a child of having two parents? Had we given enough thought to adoption? Gradually it became clear to both of us what was best for the baby. Dorothy went to a maternity home in Cincinnati, where she stayed until her son was born. She cared for him for 10 days, then signed the adoption papers—final and irrevocable.

She returned to me a thin, broken young woman. We never spoke of the baby again. Because Dorothy never mentioned him, neither did I. (I would have done anything to spare her further pain.) Eventually she found her calling working as a school librarian, where, she said, "You have the children but don't have to bother with discipline." She went door-to-door electioneering and got herself on the school board so she could do everything in her power to make sure the local kids got the best education possible. I suspected she was trying to fill the void in her life, but of course not even every child in the world could have done that. When Dorothy died in my arms from cancer, I felt what she must have felt, that aching sense of loss.

What I didn't know was that while Dorothy was alive she had spent years seeking information about her son. But the records had been sealed.

Now he's trying to contact me! I thought as I walked slowly up the drive from the mailbox. I put the letter back in the envelope and stuck it in a drawer. *Oh, Dorothy,* I thought, *if you only knew. . . .* I didn't sleep well that night, wondering how it is that God works. *Lord, your timing's all wrong,* I thought. How was I to tell if Tony really was who he claimed to be? After all these years, how would I explain him to my friends and family?

Two days later in the afternoon a neighbor dropped by for a cup of tea. I was grateful for the diversion. I was trying to keep my mind on our conversation when a forceful knock on the door nearly jolted me out of my seat. *Not now!* I thought. *It can't be him already!* Heart pounding, I opened the door, more intent on the explanation I would give my neighbor than on the tall, trim, dark-haired man in the neat business suit standing there. "Hi," he said softly. "I'm Tony."

Her eyes, her brow . . . I caught myself. "Well, look who's here," I improvised as I motioned him in. "It's Dorothy's . . . *friend* Tony. He's flown all the way from back east." I smiled at my neighbor, searching her face for signs of suspicion.

"Any friend of Dorothy's is a friend of mine," she said, and politely excused herself so we could visit. "Have a nice time, you two." As I let her out, I wondered if I wasn't crazy. Now I was alone with a complete stranger, whether he was my grandson or not. *Lord, please help me handle this.*

"Won't you sit down?" I asked. We small-talked for a while before the young man told me his story. When he and his wife decided to have children, he started to look for his birth mother, in part to determine any hereditary medical problems. "But I also wanted to know more about her." With the passage of time and legislation, the records that had been closed to the mother were made available to the son. He had been stunned and saddened to learn Dorothy had died, but heartened to find out about me.

We got comfortable with each other, and then he asked me about Dorothy. No name was sweeter to my ears, no subject dearer to my heart. I began telling him about her, though I did maintain a certain reserve. Finally, saying it was getting late, Tony left for his motel.

When I closed the door I asked myself, *What am I doing? What good could possibly come of this?*

Early the next morning Tony appeared at my door, juggling a pile of luggage. "I'm staying," he announced.

"Who says I want you to?" I shot back with a smile, not completely sure if I was kidding or not. After all, if he were an impostor, he had the perfect scheme to find out anything he wanted to know about me. But again I found myself staring and wondering how many people in this world have Dorothy's brow and eyes.

He squeezed past me and stacked his luggage inside. Tony had a million questions, asking to see pictures of Dorothy at every age. He read her poems and essays, and letters she had written me. I had saved practically everything, of course. He seemed hungry to know every detail of Dorothy's life. In spite of myself I warmed up to the young man in front of me. I went to bed feeling more comfortable with the situation. *Lord, if this is your will . . .*

The following day I awoke with a start. I grabbed my robe and hustled downstairs. I heard clanking as I approached the kitchen. Tony, wearing the gaudiest pair of gym shorts I had ever seen, was puttering around, making coffee as if he belonged there. "One thing I know about you," I said. "You're color-blind!"

Tony laughed. So did I. We laughed like old friends, and he had me, for good. I introduced my grandson to friends, neighbors, relatives, everybody I knew. No one reacted with embarrassment or disapproval. Instead, the people I care about all delighted in my good fortune.

Early that fall Tony arranged for me to fly out to visit him and his wife, who was soon to give birth. We had a fine time. Not long after I returned home Tony called. "Hey, Great-grandma!" he said, struggling for the words through his emotions. "Say hello to Louisa." I swallowed hard. A baby girl. Louisa, after Dorothy's middle name. Two months later, when Tony flew to Texas with my great-grandbaby, I almost burst with pride at the sight of her.

My health began to deteriorate, and I realized I could no longer live on my own. Tony urged me to come back east with him, but my roots were in Texas. So he returned and set me up in a charming retirement hotel. I never could have managed the move, physically or financially, without him. He takes good care of me now, just as Dorothy would have done. My grandson has enriched my life beyond measure. But far more importantly, I had tried to close the door on the past and on the pain of losing a grandson and my beloved Dorothy when there came a letter and a knock at the door.

Did I say I was too old for surprises? Not on your life. It's never too late to be surprised by the Lord's blessings.

The Old, Round Oak Table

by Isabel Wolseley

Thou preparest a table before me....
—Psalm 23:5

"Be foolish to ship that thing halfway across the country. Must weigh a ton...cost a fortune, too," said several friends.

Sound reasoning. But the old, round oak table had been in my family since long before I was born. Whenever relatives had gathered at our house, the table was pulled apart at the middle and leaves were inserted so everyone could be seated together. Grace was said at every meal, whether we had company or not.

At that table I told my parents about school happenings, sports scores, the latest boy I thought was neat. My stories—especially during my early years—were often interrupted by manners training: "Not such a big bite, Isabel." "Use your napkin, not your sleeve."

After most evening meals, my mother donned her apron—she called it her "apern"—and told me she'd "worsh" dishes while I did homework. If an arithmetic problem was a stickler, Dad sat there, too, insisting the answer must be in the back of the book; it always was when he went to school.

The table's generous forty-eight-inch top provided space for working jigsaw puzzles, or playing dominoes. Sometimes it became Mom's ironing board.

Just before bedtime, Dad would open Hulburt's *Story of the Bible* and read. Then we bowed our heads and prayed together around our old oak table.

So despite the cost, I had the table packed and shipped. Today it sits in our home, reminding me to be faithful to the things I learned at it so many years ago.

Father, help me to remember–and pass on–the values
I was taught during my growing-up years.

Making Pumpkin Pies

by Lurlene McDaniel

"Isn't that Mom's old apron? What are you doing with it, Staci?"

Eleven-year-old Staci clutched the stained white cotton apron to her chest. "Don't sneak up on me like that, Becky."

"Looks like you're the one who's sneaking," her sister Becky said, coming into the spare bedroom where boxes were stacked along the walls. Some of the boxes had been marked: ANNE'S THINGS—FOR THE GIRLS.

"I was just looking through some old stuff," Staci said defensively.

Becky touched the apron. "Mom wore this whenever she cooked. I guess Dad packed it away after her funeral." Their mother had died when Staci was eight.

"It smells sweet."

Becky sniffed the fabric. "Pie spice," she said. "She was making pumpkin pies for Thanksgiving dinner that day. I was helping her."

That day flashed back to Staci. The three of them in the kitchen. She at the table, Mom and then fourteen-year-old Becky chopping and cooking for the upcoming feast. All the relatives were coming to their house for Thanksgiving Day.

"Is that when she went to the store?" Staci asked.

Sometimes it was hard for her to remember details from three years before. And, although she had never told a soul, sometimes it was hard for her to remember her mother's face. If it hadn't been for photographs, she would have forgotten. It scared her. She didn't want to forget, but she couldn't help it.

Becky nodded. "Yes. She'd run out of some things she needed."

Staci knew the rest of the story by heart. On her way to the store, Mom's car had hit an icy patch on the road, slid into a tree. And she was killed. "That was the worst Thanksgiving ever."

Becky took Staci's arm. "Come on downstairs. Dad will be home soon and he doesn't need to find us pawing through Mom's old things."

Staci brought the apron with her, but didn't argue. Becky was home from college for the weekend and could be bossy, but she was right about Dad. Ever since that terrible Thanksgiving, Dad made sure they all did something other than celebrate the holiday at home. One year, they went camping. One year they'd gone to Disneyworld. He made sure they had fun, but Staci missed the big family get-togethers.

Becky asked, "Did he say where he plans to take us this year?"

"Not yet. But Aunt Kate invited us for Thanksgiving dinner again. She says the whole family will be coming—fifteen people."

Staci recalled vividly the day her aunt barged in and pinned her father to a chair. *"Phil,"* she said, *"you and the girls shouldn't run off this year. You're part of my sister's family and we miss all of you. Please say you'll join us."* Staci shrugged. "But Dad wouldn't promise."

In the kitchen, Becky flopped in a chair. The room looked spotless. Somehow, Staci had half expected it to be cluttered with Mom's cooking gear. She reached into the apron's oversized pocket. "I found this too." Staci held out a smudged, dog-eared index card. "It's Mom's recipe for pumpkin pie."

Becky took it. "Yeah, I remember. It was her favorite."

Her mother's handwriting looked soft and delicate.

Anne's Pumpkin Pie

(simple and yummy)

Makes 1 eight inch pie

- 1 1/4 cups cooked or canned pumpkin
- 1/4 teaspoon salt
- 1 1/4 cups milk
- 2 eggs
- 1/2 cup packed brown sugar
- 1 1/2 Tbs. granulated sugar
- 1 teaspoon cinnamon
- 1/4 teaspoon each of ginger, nutmeg and cloves

Heat oven to 425 degrees. Beat all ingredients together with rotary beater. Pour into pastry lined pan. Bake 45-55 minutes. Serve with whipped cream.

"Let's bake a pie," Staci said, suddenly overcome with an urge to make Thanksgiving feel real again.

Becky looked interested in the project, but said, "I don't even know if there's stuff around here to bake pies."

"Dad cooks a lot. Let's look."

They rummaged through the cupboards and pantry and found the necessary ingredients. "I don't know if this is such a hot idea," Becky said, eyeing the heap on the kitchen counter.

"Come on," Staci begged. "It'll be fun."

They hauled out the mixer and mixing bowls, pie pans and wooden spoons. They made a thick mound of pie dough and rolled it out just the way their mother had taught them. They mixed all the other ingredients and soon the kitchen smelled wonderful, rich and spicy.

They were laughing together when they heard the front door open. They froze when they heard their father yell, "Annie! Annie! Where are you?" He flung himself into the kitchen, a strange, wild look on his face.

For a heartbeat, no one spoke. Staci could hear the sound of her own heart thumping in the silence. "It's us, Dad," she finally said. "Me and Becky."

He sagged against the counter, his face gone pale. "I came in and smelled. . . ." He cleared his throat. "The house smelled like it used to when your mother was alive. For an instant I thought…

Staci stole a glance at Becky, who looked rooted to the floor, her eyes wide and filled with tears. Somehow, Staci knew it was up to her to explain things. She took a tiny step forward, untied the apron and held it out to him. "It's all my fault. I found Mom's old apron and the pie recipe was in the pocket. I didn't mean to upset you. I'm sorry."

"I'm not upset," he said. "It's just been such a long time since the house smelled this way." Sighing, he straightened up and tapped his coat pocket. "I bought tickets for a show in Chicago and made reservations at a nice hotel. I thought we could drive up tomorrow."

Staci's mouth felt dry, but she had to tell him the truth. "I want to go to Aunt Kate's. I miss being with everybody for Thanksgiving."

Dad looked surprised. "How about you, Becky?"

Becky nodded.

Their father rested his big hand on Staci's shoulder. "You have flour on your nose." She started to rub it off, but he stopped her. "Leave it. It reminds me of your mother." He encircled both girls and held them tightly. "I'll call your aunt and tell her we'll be there."

And all at once, a crystal clear image of her mother formed in Staci's memory. Mom was smiling and tying her apron behind her back. She blew Staci a kiss. To better keep the picture inside her mind, Staci closed her eyes and let the sweet scent of fresh-baked pumpkin pie wrap around them, like the ties of an apron. Like a hug from her mother's arms.

5

Adventures in Faith

For God hath not given us
the spirit of fear; but of power,
and of love, and of a sound mind.

— II Timothy 1:7

ALONE THROUGH THE DARK

by Ruth Hagen

I was visiting family in San Jose in August 1987 when my daughter, Judy, and 18-year-old granddaughter, Marcy, suggested we drive up to their rustic cabin in the foothills above California's San Antone Valley. Off we went, zigzagging 36 miles up and down mountain roads for the better part of the afternoon. For the last few miles the road was mostly one lane, so steep and narrow that I worried Judy's four-wheel-drive Bronco wouldn't make it. The road was a mix of powdery dirt and brittle pieces of shale on which the Bronco lurched and slid terrifyingly close to the edge of the rocky cliff.

As soon as we arrived and got inside the cabin Judy remarked with a grin that she had some good news. "The mice didn't chew through the telephone cord," she said. "And they didn't even eat our phone book." She held up the one-page sheet of local numbers, mostly those of ranchers, with no more than a dozen listings. The three of us had a chuckle as we unpacked our provisions.

The crisp mountain air gave me a good appetite, and I enjoyed Judy's supper of potatoes, sausage and peach cobbler. After we cleared the dinner dishes Marcy announced, "Mom, the water tank is pretty low. I'll take the Bronco down to the pump." All the water used in the cabin had to be hauled from down below, where there was a natural spring with a pump beside it.

I was nervous about Marcy driving that narrow dirt road so close to dark. But Judy reminded me my independent granddaughter had driven those mountain roads many times. "Remember, you've only got eight or ten inches of clearance in places," she warned as Marcy left. "Since we've had a dry spell, the roadbed is really shaky. Make sure you hug the side of the mountain."

As Marcy drove off I said a quick prayer. Judy watched her daughter's progress from the cabin's picture window, through which you could see the narrow road wind its way down the mountain.

Maybe 15 minutes passed when suddenly Judy screamed, "Oh, no! Dear God, help us!"

The cabin door slammed. Judy had taken off running. As quick as I could, I followed. "Judy, wait!"

"The Bronco went over the cliff, Momma! Come on, we have to help Marcy!"

At 78, I couldn't run as fast as Judy. She was out of sight after the first turn in the road. I ran on and on, down the hill, up the next, at least a quarter of a mile, trying to catch up. In the gathering darkness, it was getting hard to see anything ahead of me. Where had Judy gone? *God, please help me know what to do.*

Something made me stop in my tracks. I strained to see a sign of movement. There was only silence.

"Judy, where are you?" I screamed into the gathering darkness.

Down the cliff to my right I heard a frantic warning: "I'm down here, Mother! Don't come near the edge! I slipped on loose rocks and fell over. I'm down maybe twenty feet."

"Judy, what can I do?"

"Just stay back, Momma! The road is giving out all over! I think I can crawl back up. I saw the Bronco's roof as I was falling and heard Marcy calling for help. She's alive, Momma! But she's way down in the ravine. Go back to the cabin and phone for help. Tell them to send a helicopter. We've got to get Marcy out!"

I wanted to look over and make sure Judy was really okay. But I knew I might fall too, so I turned and started running back up the hill I had just tumbled down. By then I was exhausted and almost weak with panic. My heart was pounding and I was gasping. I stumbled and landed hard on my face. I tried to get up but couldn't.

I started to sob. "Dear God, please give me the strength to get back to the cabin so I can call for help."

It's hard to describe what happened then. One moment I was helpless on the ground, the next moment an electric current seemed to surge through me. I heard the words *I am here.* They were as clear as if the speaker were next to me.

I got to my feet without a wobble. When I stood, I felt relaxed and rested. A surge of pain-free energy propelled me forward. Confidently, I started to run, faster than I had before. When I reached the cabin I hurtled through the front door and called the operator.

As I sputtered out the details of the accident I realized I had no idea where I was. The cabin had no address, and I didn't know which roads led to it. In my panic I hadn't thought to ask Judy for those details. I remembered we had gone through a cattle range, but the landmarks I described to the operator only confused her. I told her to stand by and hung up. I had to get Judy to the phone so she could give directions.

I grabbed a flashlight and a walking stick. I dashed back toward Judy, but abruptly came to a fork in the road I didn't remember. Which way to go? "Lord, help me!"

Again a sense of calmness, then a reassuring certainty. *That way.* I continued to run with energy and determination. Up the hill, down the hill, up the second hill. In the shrouding darkness, I was unsure of where my loved ones were. Suddenly I sensed the right place to pause. "Marcy! Judy!" I shouted.

A faint voice filtered up from the rocks and spiky bushes below. I heard, "I'm here, Grandma." Another voice: "Momma!" It was Judy. Once again, I had stopped at the exact site of the accident. *Thank you, Lord.*

I dropped to my knees and lay flat to inch myself to the cliff's brink. Holding the walking stick over the edge, I asked Judy if she could see it was there.

"I'm coming, Momma. I'm almost there. I'm really scratched up."

I could hear gravel cascading away from where Judy was trying to climb. Minutes later I felt her grab the end of the stick. I heaved with all my strength, never imagining I could pull up my 140-pound daughter. But I did.

Judy crawled onto my lap, shaking and sweating, and immediately passed out. I held her close and stroked her forehead. "Judy, wake up. We have to get help for Marcy! Judy, wake up!" I kept talking and rubbing her head. Finally, some minutes later, she came to. I pulled her to her feet and we started walking. Dazed and bleeding, Judy fell three times as we went back to the cabin.

There, we heard the phone ringing. It was the rescue team. Judy gave them directions and we started back down the mountain to Marcy. I held on to Judy, not for my sake but for hers. She was weak, bruised and bleeding. But I was still strong enough to support her.

A half hour later fire trucks arrived, and paramedics came by helicopter. It took four hours to free Marcy from the wreckage at the bottom of the cliff. At last the local sheriff was able to pull her out the rear end of the Bronco and carry her on his back to the waiting helicopter.

Marcy was treated for a broken leg, crushed ankle, broken foot and fractured finger. The next day the sheriff came to visit her in the hospital and said, "The mountain didn't beat you. You'll be back."

No, the mountain hadn't beaten us. My granddaughter, daughter and I all have our lives to prove it.

REACTIVATE THE GIANT WITHIN YOU

by Norman Vincent Peale

It is surprising how many things get so many people down. And usually they are not the big things, the great tragedies, but rather the smaller, pesky frustrations and irritations. These seem to be the real depressants of spirit, for human beings possess deep within themselves an amazing power to meet the big issues.

For example, consider the case of Major H. P. S. Ahluwalia, of India, who climbed Everest, the highest mountain on earth. With exhilaration, he stood on that colossal peak. But now Major Ahluwalia cannot even climb from the garden to his door. He was shot in the neck by a Pakistani sniper in Kashmir, ironically after the cease-fire between the two countries was declared and hostilities had ceased. His only locomotion now is by wheelchair—this man whose powerful legs and sturdy heart carried him to the summit of the world's highest eminence.

But did this super tragedy get him down? Well, hardly. He was able to overcome a profound depression and, to use his own felicitous phrase, he "climbed the Everest within." And, explained the major, to stand on the peak of himself after struggling with his own spirit was every bit as exhilarating as the thrill of standing on the summit of the vast mountain. He dramatically demonstrated that nothing can really get a person down provided he has learned the skill, the ability, the power to keep it going.

Perhaps few will ever face a challenge to the spirit even remotely comparable to that of Major Ahluwalia. But nearly everyone has to deal with daily irritations, monotony, and those annoyances that take a toll of inspiration and motivation. To keep it going in the presence of cumulative frustrations isn't easy.

Common frustration sometimes takes uncommon expressions. There was, for example, the housewife who got fed up with the constant and unending annoyances to which she felt desperately subjected. In her inability to cope with them anymore, she set fire to the house and walked away without looking back!

Then there was the case of the quiet and submissive husband who had meekly and supinely given in for years to his irritable and nagging wife. True to his uncombative nature, the harassed man left home one morning without a word and was gone for 25 years. When he returned, his wife reported that he was much easier to get along with than before! As to his own reactions, no report was forthcoming, but this time he stayed.

The struggle with the irritations and exasperations that plague so many and the possible solutions to overcoming them were illustrated in the experience of a man from Canada. "I just could not go on," he declared. He left home without explanation. He had one objective in mind: to sign on as a deckhand on a slow freighter bound for some distant port; he did not care where.

He arrived in New York City on a Saturday to find that port activities were shut down until Monday. He wandered aimlessly, going from one movie to another, but they left him cold. On Sunday, he found himself on Fifth Avenue. There he was surprised to see crowds of people lined up to go into a church. Never before having seen a crowd queued up for church, he joined the line more in curiosity than in a desire to go to church, and he was lucky to get the last seat in the last row.

Five years later, this man wrote me to tell of his experience that Sunday morning. Looking about him, he noticed that the people were persons of various races and of all ages, lots of young people, the congregation seeming to consist of perhaps more than 50 percent men.

Everyone appeared friendly, and a strange feeling, which he finally decided to call "love plus excitement," seemed to pervade the atmosphere.

As he listened to the choir and the reading of verses from the Scriptures and the prayers, and hesitantly participated in the enthusiastic singing of old familiar hymns, he began to have a warm feeling of belonging. Memories of "the good days of my youth stirred within my mind. A profound sense of peace filled my heart. Tears came to my eyes as I sat within your great stone refuge."

The service came to a close and the big congregation began to leave the church. Everyone seemed uplifted, renewed, happy. Then the lady he had been sitting next to offered her hand in greeting and all she said was, "God loves you." That was enough. It broke him up. Out on the avenue he walked for blocks, and it was like walking on air. He knew that he could cope with anything. He drove home to Canada and was still going strong when, five years later, he wrote of the experience that taught him the dynamic truth that nothing need keep you down.

That life on earth has a powerful crushing quality can hardly be denied. Circumstances relating to health, job, money, hostility, misunderstanding, and numerous other adversaries of well-being are constantly making it difficult, if not downright painful, for multitudes of people every day. Little wonder that the psychoanalyst Sigmund Freud is reported to have said, "The chief duty of a human being is to endure life." And life can indeed be tough, very tough.

If you consider yourself weak and inadequate and lacking in power to stand up to life's challenges and rigorous difficulties, you are taking an erroneous view of yourself. You simply are not so inadequate and lacking in strength as you assume yourself to be. Indeed, such assumption is dangerous, for it tends to create the fact. You are likely to build a case against yourself if you continue such thoughts.

This results in an individual's attempts to put down the giant that the Creator has placed at the center of every personality. For there is a giant in every person, and nothing can get this giant down unless that giant is kept down by himself.

Ernie Belz had a frozen personality when he first arrived in America. He was so abnormally short of stature (only a little over four feet) that he had developed a deep-seated inferiority feeling.

A 30-year-old Swiss, who had come to the U.S. hoping to find himself, Ernie discovered it hard going at first.

His broken English usually brought a smile, and his minuscule size was always a handicap. Mounting a bus, he could not negotiate the step but had to swing himself up. When he went into a store for clothing, he was referred to the boys' department.

One day, Ernie Belz was lunching alone in a restaurant when a young man from Marble Collegiate Church invited him to our Young Adults group. He accepted and received friendship and understanding instead of the curious looks to which he was accustomed. But the thawing of a frozen personality does not happen in a day, or a month.

A big turning point came one night at a Young Adults meeting when a member spoke convincingly on the theme "God Has a Plan for My Life." Ernie had some questions about this idea. "Do I understand that you really believe God has a plan for my life, a little fellow like me?" Ernie asked doubtfully.

"Sure—God has a plan for every one of us, and this means you, too, Ernie. The problem is you must be willing to do whatever He wants you to do."

In other meetings with these spiritually alive and with-it young people, he was shown that size or color or handicap had nothing to do with how much more effective one could become.

As a result, Ernie began to think more creatively. He learned the positive principle. He stopped trying to lose himself in crowds and began to take an interest in others as individuals. He volunteered for church work projects. He also developed the art of discovering other persons' interests and bringing out the best in each individual's personality.

Good things began happening to Ernie Belz. One was that he escaped from his shell of inferiority and became a released individual. Several years later, he secured an administrative job with an educational institution in Africa.

Ernie must have grown and grown big in this job, for an executive under whom he worked wrote: "How much better this world would be if we had more people like Ernie Belz. He is a giant when it comes to helping other people find themselves."

All along, there was an undetected giant in Ernie Belz. And that giant finally emerged to disclose a man with dynamic motivation and power to keep the positive principle going and influence everyone he met. And, there is a giant in you, too. When that giant takes charge, nothing can get you down, ever. When you wholeheartedly adopt a "with all your heart" attitude and go all out with the positive principle, you can do incredible things.

What do you mean, you can't do anything? What do you mean, things get you down? Not when you have the urge, the impulse, the motivation, to everlastingly keep it going. If you think you are down, do not stay down. Get right up; shake off defeat. Reactivate the giant within you and get going and keep it going. Live always by the amazing positive principle. That is the realistic and proven philosophy that succeeds and keeps on succeeding.

But suppose you have already been knocked down and have accepted the negative thought that you are down and that you are down for good. What then? Change your attitude, really change it. Simply start affirming: "I do not mean to stay down. What an advantage to have hit bottom. I will never minimize the value of the bottom; the only direction from here is up. And up I am going."

So, start looking up. Start thinking up. Begin acting in an up manner. And keep going in an up direction, no matter how steep or how long the climb. If you keep thinking positively, affirming positively, acting positively, always practicing the positive principle, you will reach that greatly-to-be-desired top away up there. With this spirit, that top is not all that far off, and this time you will stay there, having learned how always to keep it going.

Remember:

1. Don't be concerned about your ability to handle the big disasters; shore yourself up against the little irritations and frustrations.

2. Always remember when frustrated that it isn't all that bad—and that God loves you.

3. Know for sure that there is a giant within you. And then release the giant YOU.

4. Remember and never doubt it—with God's help you can do incredible things.

5. Never think down—always think up.

6. Put problems into God's hands and leave them there. He will take care of you and bring things out right.

Fighting With All My Might

by Madge Rodda

"Another cup of coffee?" the waitress asked. Boisterous Fourth of July revelers packed the all-night restaurant on Harbor Boulevard in Costa Mesa, raising the noise level considerably in the normally quiet establishment.

I looked across the counter at the clock: 3:20 A.M.

"No, thanks," I said. "I'm running late."

Strange as it may seem, I was usually up and out at this hour on Sunday morning. I'm a church organist, and I like to get in some practice and spend time with the Lord before the early service at 7:30 A.M. The sanctuary is almost always in use, so it's difficult to find another time convenient to practice.

Before leaving the restaurant I decided to make a stop in the rest room. I went through double doors and down a long hallway into the ladies' room. One of the two stalls was occupied, and I heard the sound of paper rustling, as though someone were rifling the pages of a magazine.

I entered the other stall, and when I came out was astonished to see a tall young man blocking my way. He clamped a hand over my mouth, grabbed me by the throat and threw me to the floor. In an instant he was on top of me, pinning me to the cold tile as he loosened his belt.

I was a 69-year-old grandmother, an inch under five feet in height, 115 pounds, and no match for a strong young man. But I flailed and punched for all I was worth. "Lord, help me!" I screamed.

His rough hands tightened around my throat. Wriggling and kicking, I managed to shove him off and scramble to my feet. Frantic, I broke free and managed to pull the door to the hall open. Furiously he slammed it and pulled me to the floor so hard that my shoes flew off. He wedged something beneath the door to keep it from opening.

"Lord, save me!" Why didn't someone come to help me? My cries must not have been heard. My assailant snapped my head to the right, then the left, twisting hard. Was he trying to break my neck? I kicked against his legs.

Suddenly he pushed his thumbs deep into my throat. Long frenzied minutes passed as he tried to batter me into submission. But each time he slammed me to the floor, I somehow was able to keep him from overpowering me. As terrified as I was, I felt a strange sense of strength and calm. God's presence in that room was as real as my attacker's.

I wrenched free and pushed hard, again managing to stand. But he sprang up and twisted me as if I were a doll. I continued to struggle and cry out, "Lord, save me!" He covered my nose and mouth again and pushed me to the floor. I squirmed and clawed and kicked ferociously. Enraged, he took out a knife.

Images of my three daughters flashed through my mind. Suzanne, Melanie, and Rosalee. I didn't want to leave them. My two grandsons, Kevin and Connor, were only three and one. I couldn't miss out on their lives. I had to keep fighting. I had to stay alive. As I jerked away from my attacker, I felt the knife slice my neck.

Blood covered my chest; my white blouse turned deep red. I stopped fighting. "Dear Jesus," I gasped, "only you can save me."

The man let go of me. He got to his feet, breathing hard, and began to pace between me and the door. "The time has come!" he shouted, still gripping the knife. "The time has come!" He chanted the words over and over, gazing around the tiny space with glazed eyes. He grabbed my purse and rifled through it.

Suddenly the door rattled. Someone knocked and pushed against it. I tried to cry out but could barely whisper. In a second all became quiet again.

"Give me money," my assailant snapped as he threw my purse at me.

With shaking hands I fumbled for my wallet, offering the 20 or so dollars inside. He snatched the bills. One of my knee-high stockings had come off during the struggle, and he pulled it over his head to hide his face. He yanked the door open, but then he stopped, turned and spoke again. They were words I had hardly expected to hear.

"I believe in God too," he said. "But Satan is poisoning my mind. I need help. I know I need help."

The door slammed. He was gone.

Numb, I lay in a pool of blood. In a few seconds the door flew open. The manager and a waitress stared at me in horror.

"Call an ambulance and the police!" the manager shouted. The waitress rushed to press towels and cold packs against my neck, then helped me struggle to a booth inside the dining area. Other employees and customers did what they could to help. In a blur, I saw it was nearly 3:45 A.M.

A policeman appeared. "The manager chased and caught a guy running away," he said. "Are you able to look through the window and tell me if that's the man who attacked you?"

I could see my assailant just outside, held tight by two policemen. "Yes, that's the man," I rasped. Then paramedics arrived and rushed me to the emergency room.

My daughter Rosalee and one of our pastors joined me at the hospital. Rosalee later told me I was so swollen and battered she didn't recognize me. Now we waited to see if I would need surgery. Joining hands, we silently prayed. Suddenly the attacker's words—"I need help"—returned to my mind. "That poor man," I murmured, not realizing I had spoken out loud.

"Mom, who are you talking about?" asked Rosalee.

"Why, the man who attacked me." To my own surprise, I said a prayer that the powerful love that had just saved my life would change *his*.

I received stitches for my throat wound and treatment for my multiple cuts and bruises. The knife had narrowly missed my carotid artery. Counselors told me I would need therapy to help me get over the trauma. "The Lord has taken care of that already," I told them. "Just as He took care of me throughout my ordeal."

Weeks later I found I was thinking more and more about the young man's final words to me. "I need help," he had said. I prayed, asking what the Lord would have me do to help him.

Such an impulse was not my own. I could be pretty good at harboring a grudge, and if ever I had reason it was now. Who would blame me if I gloated over whatever punishment my assailant received, or if I hauled him though the courts in a bitter demand for damages?

But God was telling me to reach out. My attacker—a transient from Texas who was in town with a carnival—had been high on cocaine. He had said he needed help, and I knew where he could get it. How could I refuse?

It was March 1993 when the case came to trial and the young man was sentenced to 17 years in prison. At the trial's close, with the judge's permission, I gave the prisoner a Bible, with passages marked that I hoped would start him on the road to finding the help he needed. I also assured my attacker that I had forgiven him.

To the question "Why?" I have only one answer: There isn't any one of us who isn't a sinner somewhere along the line, and when I think of the price Jesus paid to forgive me of my sins, how could I possibly not forgive anyone else?

Some have wondered if God's presence *really* enabled me to survive such a vicious attack. "Do I look as if I could engage in mortal combat for at least fifteen minutes without divine intervention?" I say with a smile. "If you think so, I'd like to sell you the Brooklyn Bridge, because you'd believe anything!"

On the Way to Damascus

by Chris Clark Davidson

We made two mistakes that day: venturing out on the roads after a heavy snowfall before the plows could finish their work, and worse, risking a lightly traveled shortcut. Those mistakes might have cost us too, if it hadn't been for two ordinary-looking young men and their truck.

It had started out as a simple trip to visit my grandmother, who lived alone. Mom and I wanted to check on her after the storm and take her grocery shopping. So we piled into my car with my sons—toddler Phillip and baby Joseph—for the two-hour trip to Damascus, Pennsylvania.

The first leg went uneventfully enough . . . until I decided to save some time by using a connecting road between highways, rather than sticking to the interstate. The road was narrow, with snow piled high on either side, and when a car going the other way veered into our lane, I had no choice but to jerk the wheel to the right. We ended up in a snowbank while the driver continued on, apparently oblivious to our predicament. Even though we had pretty good nubs on our winter-treads, the wheels whined and spun uselessly when I tried to pull out. *Now what'll I do, Lord?* I wondered as I tucked

Joseph's blanket up around his chin in the car seat. *Please give us a hand.*

The bad weather had kept away the truck traffic that usually traversed this road. We hadn't seen a single car besides the one that ran us into the snowbank. I noticed a silo and a barn roof above the bare trees about a quarter mile down the road at the end of a field.

"Mom, I'm going to see if I can get help at that farm up ahead." Before starting out I made sure no snow blocked the tailpipe so I could leave the engine running to warm the car. "Be careful, dear," Mom said as I set off.

I hadn't thought to wear boots, and my feet were wet and freezing as I slogged down the road. By the time I reached the barn I was shivering. I had grown up on a farm, so I easily—and gratefully—recognized this as a working dairy. When I swung open the milkhouse door, a welcome blast of moist heat hit me in the face and my glasses fogged up. As I took them off to wipe the lenses, I noticed a spinning fan in the opposite window keeping the air circulating.

I cautiously headed toward the voices I heard several stalls away. I say cautiously because fresh manure splattered the floor and I had to tread with care.

The voices belonged to two brawny young men who were horsing around more than working, though their attire identified them as farmhands: dusty denim overalls, work boots and heavy flannel shirts. "Hi," I greeted them hesitantly. They stopped and smiled, instantly putting me at ease. The two listened obligingly while I explained my situation, then one fellow said, "Stay here." With that he bounded out of the barn. The next thing I knew I heard a horn honking. The man had returned driving a blue pickup, a late model like my husband's, and by the mud

spatters and a few dings, clearly well used. "Get in!" he called while his companion held the door, helped me up, then slid in after me in the front seat.

We roared down the drive and onto the road, taking only a minute or so to reach my car. I waved to Mom and the boys while the two men looked out the windshield. "Yep, she's stuck all right!" the driver said. The passenger concurred. With that, the driver mashed down the accelerator and we barreled out into the field! He did a wide doughnut, the truck sending up a rooster tail of snow as we spun around. Both men were grinning as we bounced back onto the road with the truck now in a position to pull my car out. "Do you always drive like this?" I asked, a little surprised by their bravado.

"Shucks," the driver replied, "it ain't our truck."

The passenger jumped out, grabbed a chain from the back and in a minute we were unstuck and ready to continue on our way to Grandma's. Before we did, though, I thanked the young strangers and offered them some money, but they declined, saying, "It was our pleasure, ma'am."

Just two weeks later, when winter was pretty much over, Mom and I were on our way down the same road to visit Grandma. I decided to stop and thank the two men once more and let them know that we had made it safely to Damascus that day. I was in for the shock of my life.

The barn was empty. In fact, it was dilapidated. The whole operation was in such a state of neglect and disrepair that it was clear the farm hadn't been used in quite some time. The hinges on the milkhouse door were busted. The fan was bent and rusted. I couldn't understand it. Just two weeks before. . . .

I checked with the woman at the next house down the road. "No," she assured me, "that farm has been abandoned for years."

I got back in the car. How could this be? I stared at Mom, who assured me that this was where we had gotten stuck and found help. *I know this is the place.*

Then I smiled and slipped the car in gear. I had asked the Lord to give us a hand. He had given us two—a pair of sturdy young farmhands who helped us out and had a little fun while they were at it, doing some joyriding in the Boss's truck.

He Kept His Promise

by Hubbard Keavy

On June 7, 1945, Danny Davey was at his battle station as an anti-aircraft gunner aboard a U.S. carrier, cruising near Okinawa.

Suddenly, coming straight over the stern was a Japanese kamikaze plane with two bombs. The plane hit three decks below. Danny was knocked off his seat. When he came to and realized he was in one piece, the 19-year-old made a promise: If I ever have a chance to save lives, I will.

By war's end, Danny had been in 13 battles, but never got a scratch. And he never forgot his promise to "The Man Upstairs."

In 1948, soon after he was hired as a driver for United Parcel Service in Laguna Beach, California, Danny began devoting his spare time to bettering the lives of thousands of Hopis and Navajos in Arizona.

For the next 47 years, when he wasn't with his wife and two sons, Danny spent his time, energy and talent as a scrounger to fulfill his vow. He drove 10,000 miles a year, sleeping about five hours a night and spending 20 a hours week picking up donations. He spent a week on reservations at Easter, Thanksgiving and Christmas.

On his trips, Danny had to contend with snow and sub-zero cold, angry desert dust, flash floods, flat tires, and broken-down trucks. Nothing could cool his ardor.

Call it luck, coincidence or God's grace, happenstances have helped Danny's mission mightily: A millionaire heard about Danny and built him a warehouse. A group of flyers known as the Skylarks once flew 33 planes loaded with goods to Arizona.

In 1971, Danny's project became the non-profit Thunderbird Foundation. Thanks to volunteers, its administrative costs are zero. To enlist volunteers, gather goods, and raise funds, Danny makes slide presentations to gatherings, large and small.

Since he retired from UPS in 1988, Danny spends even more time helping his friends. Undoubtedly, with the food, blankets, clothing, medicine and other necessities he has delivered, Danny Davey has kept his vow to save lives.

Says Danny: "My greatest rewards are having a family that understands, and knowing that the recipients are grateful."

A Night Landing in the Dark

by Peggy M. Pryor

As my husband and I drove past the lake toward the little airport, the dreary day seemed to match my anxiety. *Maybe the weather will be too bad for flying,* I thought as I looked at low clouds pushing across the winter sky.

Glancing at James's strong profile, I tried to let go of my fears. I had always felt safe with him before. Yet I was still apprehensive. *If only he had flown more in the past year,* I thought.

James's flying lessons had been sporadic. We owned three clothing shops and had just opened a fourth. Time was a rationed commodity for us. But nearly every afternoon during the previous month James had practiced for his flight test. As I listened from the store I heard the dull drone of a plane, and I always breathed a prayer for his safety.

It had been only a week since he had returned from the airport with achievement and satisfaction in his eyes, and immediately I knew he was a licensed pilot. And today he would experience a new satisfaction—his first flight ever with a passenger.

The dismal morning had turned into the kind of Mississippi day that mocks the winter calendar. A gentle breeze stirred, and the temperature had risen to 60 degrees. At the airport we were greeted with a friendly smile from Tommy Patterson, the airport manager, who was also James's flight instructor. "Hope you don't mind, James, but I had to service the Skyhawk for you," he said. "The Cherokee had already been reserved."

I knew James had never flown a Skyhawk. Suddenly I felt more than a little apprehension.

"He'll have to take the plane up alone twice and come in for two landings before you can fly with him, Peggy." Tommy turned to James, and as they walked away I heard him continue in a low voice, "Just keep your head, James. This plane shouldn't give you any trouble."

I didn't feel so sure. In fact, I was ready to ditch the whole idea. But it was three weeks before Christmas, and we were low on men's suits in the stores. The trip to the factory in Tupelo had to be made. *This is ridiculous,* I thought, determined to enjoy the trip.

I relaxed somewhat after James finished his second landing. Within minutes I was beside him, our seat belts were fastened, and with a lurch of my heart, we were airborne. Watching the airport disappear, I realized my fears were disappearing also, and I settled down to a surprisingly pleasant flight.

As we approached Tupelo, James asked me to help him locate the airport. He was flying visually, following highways, towns and rivers. Landings had always frightened me. When we spotted the airport, I didn't want to look as we descended toward the runway. I closed my eyes and suddenly we were down.

As a taxi carried us to the factory, James again reminded me to speed up my buying, for we had to be back at the airport no later than four o'clock that afternoon. The trip home would take about an hour, and darkness came in earnest by 5:30 P.M. James did not have to remind me he had never flown after dark, or indeed that he had had no instrument training for night flying.

The factory was crowded and the personnel were overworked; the day became one giant effort to buy the suits and be on our way. Finally at 3:30 P.M. the suits were all boxed at the freight door and our cab had been called.

We waited . . . and waited. No cab arrived even after repeated calls to the company. Four o'clock came, the time we had said we must be at the airport. Then 4:15 P.M. Even James had become more than a little upset, all the while assuring me we could get home before dark if we left at 4:30 P.M. Finally, at 4:20 P.M., cab drove into the loading zone and a surly driver glared at our bulging boxes. Between his reluctant efforts and our almost frantic ones, we were finally loaded and headed south toward the airport.

The warm sunny day had settled into a dismal chilling dusk—the time of a winter day that always reminded me of a tired old man making his way home. At the airport the little plane looked smaller and older as I watched James check it over before departure.

We were airborne before I glanced at my watch—and then was sorry I had looked. It was already five o'clock. Darkness would surround us in about 30 minutes. I watched the lights coming on in the city below us.

Now we were alone. Not a word was spoken. The only sound was the whir of the engine, which I hoped masked the thumping of my heart. Without turning my head, I wondered if James's hands were trembling at the controls.

As dusk turned to night, I realized we were probably only halfway home. From time to time the darkness gave way to lonely lights of houses, then to dozens of less lonesome lights clustered together in towns. Knowing we must find our way home by following familiar sights, I searched for signs of our location, but could not bring myself to ask questions.

Time passed. As my eyes strained, I barely made out a lighter area below. We were over water. That must be Grenada Lake, which meant we were near the airport and would be seeing the runway lights soon. But my momentary relief disintegrated almost before it came as I thought of the approaching night landing.

James's words pierced the silence. "Look below you, to your right, and help me find the airport lights. And don't worry. We'll be fine." The words were convincing. The voice was not.

As I searched the darkness below, broken by occasional lights, I could see no signs of the airport.

Without waiting for my answer, James began the radio conversation that filled me with sheer terror.

"Grenada Radio, this is Cessna N17954. Over."

"Cessna 17954, this is Grenada Radio."

"This is 17954. What's wrong with the runway lights?"

Silence. And then the shocking words: "We have a malfunction in the runway lights. You'll have to land without them. Do you think you can make it?"

No runway lights! Never in my worst fears would I have imagined this. Suddenly I was certain we would crash. I reached out in desperation to touch James's hand—and felt it tremble. I forced my eyes to look downward, straining in the darkness for signs of the airport. Then, without warning, I saw shadows of trees and buildings ahead, and I knew we were descending.

And just as suddenly, the plane banked to the right and began to rise above the shadows, toward the dark winter sky.

I thought of our three children and wondered how David, our youngest, would manage without his parents. I was aware only of my heart pounding, my body shaking, and tears wetting my cheeks.

I jumped as James spoke. "We're going in this time. And we'll be fine." His words did not stop my terror, but they must have shocked me into reality. I began to pray. "Oh, God, I don't want to die! But if it is your will, then please open the gates of heaven for James and me!"

Following that prayer I began to feel at peace, and then in that moment of complete trust I knew God's hands were on James's at the controls of the plane. We were still circling the airport, but I was no longer afraid. As surely as life itself, I knew we were safe! It must have taken another five minutes before we descended, but finally the plane rolled to a smooth stop at the end of the dark runway.

As we drove home, the temperature dropped to 30 degrees. But I rolled down the car window and smiled as the cold wind blew my hair. The dark sky above now seemed set with diamonds. And as I watched the twinkling stars so near to heaven, it seemed to me the entire universe was vibrating with God's promise, "And, lo, I am with you always."

Assurance

by Brigitte Weeks

"I tell you the truth, I have not found anyone in Israel with such great faith."
—Matthew 8:10 (NIV)

I woke up with a slight feeling of unease. What was wrong? Oh, yes, I remembered too quickly. Today, my three children were setting out on a canoe trip up the Napo river in the Amazon Basin to explore the rain forest. At 23, 21 and 20, it was a great adventure, the greatest adventure of their lives. They had saved and planned, chattering about piranha fishing, butterfly farms, monkeys, bug sprays, rubber boots and flashlights.

Now they were gone. And I was in New York City with absolutely no way of reaching them. *If only they had a cellular phone*, I thought, *or a fax machine*. A fax machine in the rain forest! That was pretty silly, even for an anxious mom. But I just wanted some proof that they were all right, that they were together, not lost or separated, or hacking their way through the steamy green jungle far from rescuers.

"Wait a minute," I said to myself. Words from Matthew 8:8 (NIV) I had read only a few days before came back to me: "Just say the word, and my servant will be healed," the worried Roman soldier said to Jesus, Who replied, "It will be done just as you believed it would." The centurion didn't ask Jesus to take time from His busy schedule to go to his house and heal the sick man. He didn't whip out his cellular phone to check if a miracle had indeed happened. He asked for no proof, only for Jesus' assurance that all would be well.

Where did that Roman Centurion two thousand years ago find such faith in an unknown teacher in what was for him a foreign land? I took a deep breath, looked myself in the eye and said aloud, "Jesus, please keep a close watch on the Amazon River basin today," got dressed and went to work. Honestly, my thoughts that day in quiet moments were only of adventure and learning, not of threats and danger.

The children (young persons, I should say) came back whole and I am now the proud owner of a very sinister-looking piranha skull.

Lord, help me to remember that faith in You is
the best answer to anxiety.

Trouble on Turkey Creek Bridge

by Steve Alligood

There are lots of things I like about living in Georgia, but sometimes I wish we got tons of snow like the kids who live up north do. I remember, though, one day when we got more than enough of the frosty white stuff.

I was 12 at the time, and my mom had been going to see my grandmother every day. Grandma was in the hospital and really sick. So even when we woke up one morning to a world of snow, Mom knew she had to make the ten-mile trip. She couldn't bear the thought of Grandma being alone. I decided to ride along with her.

The worst thing about snow in Georgia is that it's so rare, no one is ever prepared for it. Most people don't own snow tires, and the towns aren't equipped to plow the roads properly. So things can get pretty dangerous.

Highway 80 was down to a single lane, with snow banked up on both sides. We crept down the hill that led to Turkey Creek Bridge. As we started across, I looked behind us. At the top of the hill, a huge 18-wheeler began its descent. "Go faster, Mom," I said. "There's a big truck right behind us!" I could feel the car's wheels spinning under us on the icy path. "He's gaining!" I warned. Mom and I both looked for a place to pull over. There was none. Four-foot-high drifts touched the bridge railings, trapping us in the single lane.

We started praying—hard. We were in the middle of the bridge now, with that truck coming on faster and faster. We were sure to be flattened.

Then, suddenly, the 18-wheeler was ahead of us. *Ahead* of us! Mom drove to the end of the bridge and stopped the car. We cheered in relief and thanksgiving. We'd made it! The snowbanks were still there, just the way they'd been. No tracks of anything passing us, and yet it *had*.

Since then, Turkey Creek Bridge has been widened. But I'll never forget that snowy day God heard our prayers and widened it, temporarily, just for us.

6 Witness to Glory

The heavens declare the glory of God; and firmament showed his handiwork.

— Psalm 19:1

THE BLUE ANGELS

by William Gillies Kalaidjian

Right or wrong, a lot of cops think no one understands them except another cop. No one but a fellow officer can identify with the incredible pressures of the job—the lonely fear of a midnight foot patrol or the frenzied terror of a high-speed freeway chase; the stress of deciding in a split second whether a drug-crazed teenager is pointing a toy gun or a real one; the worry about what will happen to our families should we make the ultimate sacrifice in the line of duty. Cops like to count on each other first and foremost.

As a chaplain with the New York City Police Department for four decades, I have been both cop and confidant. I've been there with a cop's family in the emergency room, waiting for the surgeon to tell us if the officer was going to survive his wounds. I've comforted a patrolman who shot an armed robber and felt terrible about having harmed another human being. And I've attended too many funerals for good men and women who died before their time.

I started my career as a foot patrolman, following a stint in the Navy. Meanwhile I studied for the ministry at Adelphi College and then Union Theological Seminary. After my ordination I was installed as pastor of Bedford Park Congregational Church in the

Bronx. But I missed the force and my fellow officers. When the opportunity came to work for the department as a chaplain, I took it.

Being a police chaplain and a full-time pastor hasn't given me a lot of free time through the years, but on a muggy summer night in 1991 I was enjoying a rare evening of relaxation on the porch of our house on 201st Street in the Bronx. As usual I had my portable police radio close at hand, in case I was needed. When I thought I saw a man trying the doors of parked cars lining the still, dark street, I stood up. *Better check it out,* I thought, grabbing my radio. Maybe someone was trying to break into cars. Schools had let out for the year and sometimes kids got into trouble on hot nights.

I proceeded cautiously. Not even the ghost of a breeze disturbed the clammy air. My fingers tightened around the radio as I walked down to the street. If I observed a suspect entering a car, my next move would be to radio a code 10-85 and request quick backup.

Sweat beaded my brow and my clothes clung to me. Stock-still, I stood at the curb. In the dead silence I could hear my heart beating. The thought crossed my mind that I must look awfully vulnerable, standing alone on a dark street. Then, swooshing out of the night, a late-model sedan skidded to a halt directly alongside me. Before I could react, a man leapt out, muscles rippling, and assumed a military crouch. He trained a double-barreled shotgun directly on me and hissed, "Don't move."

I didn't. I barely breathed. The driver, a huge fellow, rushed up and tried to tear off my wristwatch. "Give me your wallet, man," he snarled, shoving me. "Hurry up."

I don't know what got into me. I would normally be the first to say that you should never, ever resist a mugger. Compliance is the safest bet. That's what we always tell civilians. Cash and jewelry are not worth your life. If I had to do it over again, I would just hand over my wallet. But for some reason, that night I got mad. Really mad.

I whacked the thug with my radio. He cursed me, enraged. I swung at him again and he charged me like a mad bull, hurling me into a fence nearby. I hit with a thud. Air exploded out of my lungs. I heard him scream at his partner, "Shoot him! Kill him!" I waited for the two big muzzles to blaze and shotgun pellets to rip through me.

Bullets travel faster than sound, and as any cop who survives a shooting will tell you, you feel the bullet before you hear the shot. But I felt and heard nothing. I looked skyward and immediately saw the most awesome sight of my life—a phalanx of policemen. They hovered above, standing out against the dark Bronx sky. A legion of blue-uniformed men, shoulder to shoulder in close deep ranks, shoes spit-polished, sterling shields and silver wings gleaming. Angels on patrol, heavenly cops to the rescue.

I thought quickly, *Yea, though I walk through the valley of the shadow of death, I will fear no evil,* and all fear left me. I felt as though I were standing with God. My attackers seemed to be frozen in place. Words came to me silently but forcefully: *Call for backup. Now!*

Radio in hand, I looked the perpetrator directly in the eye and pressed the call button. "This is the police chaplain," I shouted. "10-13 at 201st and Bainbridge, 10-13, 10-13!" The 10-13 code would alert every cop in the borough that a fellow officer was in trouble. Almost instantly the night erupted with screaming sirens. To my ears it was a symphony. As the angels above faded, patrol cars converged on Bainbridge Avenue, lights flashing. My attackers dove into their town car and tore off down the street, tires squealing. I jumped in the back of the first squad car that swooped up and we took off in hot pursuit. We lost them but put out an APB on their tags. In less than half an hour the men were taken into custody. Eventually they were sentenced to hard time upstate.

Three years later I still counsel cops and try to help them when they need the understanding they might not easily find outside the department. Nothing is more reassuring to a police officer than knowing he can get backup when he's in trouble, that other cops will be there when he calls. I know. I found out for myself one hot night in the Bronx, when God sent in his backup.

Serenade at Sunrise

by Janice Brooks-Headrick

I had never been more homesick or stressed than that Christmas in 1981, the year my husband Charles and I pulled up stakes and moved to the Texas badlands to work in the vast oil fields of the panhandle. We were thousands of miles away from home for the first time. Our relationship was young, so we didn't have the comfort of long years of habit to smooth over the lumps in life. Money was tight. If I hadn't been madly in love with the man with the turquoise-blue eyes, I would have run home to Mama. As it was, I cried every time I heard "White Christmas."

Charles had three children from a previous marriage who came along to live with us—Charlie, 15, Sherri, 14, and Kresti, 9. All were sick for a full three months after the move—measles, chicken pox, tonsillitis. They grew out of clothes faster than they grew into them. Then there was Charles's brother Jim. A gifted musician, Jim had rolled through from the West Coast on his way to Nashville. He stopped in the café where I waited tables and said he would be in town for a few days, sleeping in his car. I offered him our couch. Four months later, Jim was still on the couch.

With six mouths to feed, house and car payments, doctor bills and what have you, we worked countless hours just to make ends meet. One night I woke up crying. I didn't know how to work any harder, any smarter, or make any more money to afford a good old Christmas like back home. This year we just wouldn't *have* Christmas. It broke my heart.

Not long after, Jim came in from his job at a shop where he repaired drilling equipment to say there was a fellow who needed his wells watched during Christmas. Wells have to be watched when workers aren't around, and they would all be off for the holiday. If the generators go on the blink, the wells can explode. Besides, this fellow had had some tools and expensive equipment turn up missing and he suspected thieves had been sneaking around.

Charles, Jim and I had a quick conference around the kitchen table. "If we take the work," Charles said, "we can afford to celebrate a few days early. Then we'll watch the wells in shifts on Christmas Eve and Christmas, with one of us always here to keep an eye on the kids."

That's how I came to be guarding an oil well my first Christmas Eve in Texas.

Charles's job was to baby-sit the gas well. It needed a practiced eye because gas wells can blow sky-high if anything goes wrong. Jim and I split shifts at the big oil well. He drove me out for my shift with the kids and my feisty keeshond Foxy crammed in the backseat. I had been told there was a trailer with phone, electricity, radio, TV and flush toilets. Still I was nervous. That's why I was bringing Foxy along, as well as the .22 in my purse. I was worried about those thieves. We were jouncing along when Charlie hollered, "Look!"

In the black-velvet sky shone a single dazzling star. Yes, like everything else in Texas, stars are *big*. But I had never seen anything like the brilliance of that star in the eastern sky. It was the size of my fist. "You think that's the same star the wise men saw?" Charlie wondered aloud. For an instant it really felt like Christmas.

My joy faded, though, when we bounced into the oil well site. It's hard to convey the size, smell and roar of a Texas oil rig. The drilling floor was almost five stories off the ground! Jim went over the checklist with me for the monstrous generators. Set inside a building, they reeked of fuel and made a noise like their name: Waukeshaws. *Wa-kee-sha . . . wa-kee-sha . . .* Even with our bulky ear protectors the noise still drummed into my bones.

A vast waste pit contained drainage from the rig. The stench of oil permeated everything. It was about as far from the Norman Rockwell Christmas of my dreams as I could have imagined.

Jim dropped me and Foxy off at the trailer. "See you tomorrow," he said as he and the kids drove off. "Merry Christmas!"

I tried to settle in. I had brought some sewing to do and some snacks. I turned on the TV but reception was bad this far from a transmitter. I thought of my relatives back in Tennessee—cousins, brothers, sisters, nephews, uncles, aunts—all having a joyous Christmas Eve together. I grabbed the phone, thinking to call my folks in New York. *At least we can cry together,* I told myself. The phone was dead.

I hoped robbers wouldn't be out on Christmas Eve. I had Foxy, who would bristle, snarl and snap if there was trouble, though I didn't think she had it in her to attack. Well, I could shoot the thieves—if I had it in me. I checked the pistol. No bullets. Great. I was 30 miles from help, with no car, a phone that didn't work, a dog that wouldn't bite, and a gun that couldn't shoot. *Lord,* I prayed, *please don't forget about me all alone out here.*

It was a good thing I had brought the sewing. The generators wouldn't need checking until morning. I sewed until my eyelids got heavy, then bundled up and went to sleep.

I awoke to dawn drifting in the windows. Sunrise in the desert is wondrous, the colors amplified by the stark landscape. Texans say when God was making the world he ran out of mountains, trees and rivers by the time he got to the Texas badlands. So he just emptied his paint box and gave them the most glorious sunsets and sunrises on earth. I think it takes that kind of desolation to make room for so much beauty.

As a bonus, my favorite Christmas hymn, "Joy to the World!" was playing on the radio. Smiling sleepily, I reached to turn it up and was quite surprised I couldn't. The radio wasn't playing. It wasn't even plugged in.

"He rules the world. . . ."

It sounded like a huge choir, the soaring voices blending perfectly. I looked at the TV. It too was off. I got up and unplugged it anyway.

Still the choir rang out, even over the thrum of the Waukeshaws. It seemed like the sound was coming from everywhere at once.

"And makes the nations prove. . . ."

I searched the trailer. There was no radio, no TV, no tape player to account for the ringing chorus of joyous voices. I knew the song by heart and could understand every word the choir sang. Sound carries far in the desert, but 30 miles? Impossible. *It must be coming from outside.*

I wrapped my coat around me and stepped out into the sharp morning air. Foxy was dancing circles around my ankles, her ears at the alert. We looked and looked for a source. The music seemed to be coming from the east . . . from *all* of the east.

"No more let sins and sorrows grow. . . ."

Was there someone on the other side of the pit? Jim blasting the car radio to wake me up? Foxy and I climbed an embankment. We were completely alone with the most awesome sunrise I had ever seen, even for Texas. The midnight-blue of the sky lightened into vivid colors that spilled across the desert—lilac, cerulean, magenta, sienna.

I sat on the cold, sandy bank, my arm around Foxy, awash with music and light. There were no other intrusions on my senses—no sounds, no smells. Maybe I was hallucinating. Maybe I was reacting to stress and loneliness. When the verses were over, no doubt, the music would fade. But then something happened, something I still can't explain.

The voices swelled into a fourth verse of "Joy to the World!" I knew only three verses. Still, I was hearing a fourth as clear as the day that was dawning, with the full force of the invisible cosmic serenade. I cannot remember the words to that verse. They were rich with praise and glory, I know, and clear to me at the time. But today I cannot repeat a single line. (I've checked hymnbooks and discovered a fourth verse—though not the one I heard that morning!) Like the colors of that dawn sky, the words were both tangible and intangible, meant only for the moment yet leaving an impression for a lifetime.

A heavenly host sang that morning out in a Texas oil field. I thought I was alone and forgotten, forced to endure the most desolate Christmas of my life. But God shook me awake with an unforgettable reminder that His glory and the glory of His son are everpresent.

"Go to the Hospital"

by Frances G. Kjerner

As Christmas neared, I had determined to turn down several dinner invitations from friends who had been so kind to me after my husband died and had left me with no family here on the eastern shore of Virginia.

About midnight on Christmas Eve, I said to the Lord that Christmas was almost here, and I was not sure what I should do on this special day. Immediately, as if I heard a telephone ring in my head, a voice said, "Go to the hospital."

The next morning, I went to our local hospital and offered my service as a volunteer on Christmas Day to visit patients who had no family to come to see them. I was asked to be there from 10 A.M. to 2 P.M. and would have dinner in the cafeteria.

On my way to the hospital Christmas Day, I could hardly believe my eyes when three deer crossed the road in front of my car. When I began my rounds to various patients' rooms and introduced myself, I told them that Santa Claus had left three of his reindeer on shore last night. It made a nice introduction to the people who didn't know me.

By 2 P.M., I had visited many patients on four floors of the hospital and had enjoyed every minute.

I returned home and unwrapped my presents. Later, I opened a can of soup and decided that it was a very satisfactory way for a 92-year-old widow to spend this special day.

And, I didn't have to go on a diet the next day to work off the fat!

Since that day, I have volunteered every Thanksgiving and Christmas at the hospital.

It's a tradition I highly recommend.

My True Confession

by Paul Galanti

I was lashed to a wooden stool in an unheated interrogation room at what we American POWs ruefully called the Hanoi Hilton. The ropes binding my hands behind me cut deep into my wrists. On the floor a few feet in front of me was a bowl of watery gruel in a rusted, lopsided tin. This was day 10 of another period of torture and interrogation.

By then, January 1969, I had been a prisoner of the North Vietnamese for two and a half years after being shot down during my ninety-seventh combat mission. After I ejected from my crippled Navy Skyhawk attack bomber, an enemy bullet had caught me in the neck while I dangled helplessly from my parachute. Captured, I had been forced to march for 12 days to the prison in Hanoi. There the process of breaking me down began, as it did for all American POWs, with trying to force me to sign a written confession of my "war crimes." I was brutally beaten and psychologically tortured. Still, like most of my compatriots, I refused to sign.

I eyed the battered tin, as did the rats in the grimy, freezing room. To eat, I had to rock my stool until it fell forward. Then, like a starving animal, I would lap up my one daily ration of gruel, hoping the guard outside wouldn't wait too long before coming in and pulling me upright again, lest the rats eat the dribbles of food off my chin. But this was a respite. Sooner or later another torture session would begin.

Torture could last hours at a time. They used a rope contraption to twist my limbs into pretzellike contortions, tightening the restraints until the agony was beyond unbearable and the only reality was the stupefying pain. When my mind drifted, my captors' shouts and slaps penetrated the haze, bringing me back.

Worse in some ways was the time between interrogations. Dragged back to my dingy cell, I languished in cramped isolation for months. I was forbidden to speak with my fellow prisoners, communicating only sporadically by whispering and surreptitious tapping in code on the walls. The days passed mostly in silence. I spent hours trying to keep myself sane by formulating to the minutest detail all the grand business schemes I planned to carry out after the war. Sometimes I watched what we called Hanoi racing spiders, big furry things that could actually rout the rats and devour the lizards that sped over the rough, clammy walls.

I couldn't take my eyes off the gruel. I knew I needed its paltry nourishment to endure another round of barbarous punishment in the interrogation room, but I could not bring myself to fall over and lap it up. I tried to pray for strength. *Dear Lord . . .*

Even quasi-religious types like me turned to prayer regularly in the Hanoi Hilton. I was the son of a highly decorated Army colonel and had attended ecumenical chapels at bases all over the world for most of my life. But faith had never meant much to me. I was more interested in the hard-living, girl-chasing image that fighter pilots cultivated. I toned that down when I married Phyllis, but religion was still pretty much just a Sunday-morning kind of thing for me.

On Sunday mornings at the Hanoi Hilton, though, I at last made a deep connection with faith. None of us could afford to turn his back on God. Three deliberate, commanding thumps on the wall were the signal for all of us to stand for services. Alone in our cells, we said the Lord's Prayer and then the Pledge of Allegiance, our voices mingling in the narrow passageway outside.

Now, awaiting the return of my tormentors and trying to gather an appetite for the cold slop in the dirty pan, I felt I couldn't go on, even with God's help. I was too weak, too broken. I would never sign a confession, but I couldn't endure much more of this agony. What was the sense of eating? I was dying anyway, dying from the inside out, not just from the pain but from the utter senselessness of it. I was at a point where it seemed almost a crime to go on living. I wouldn't eat. I would die instead.

At that instant of spiritual and psychological checkmate, slumped on my stool, I experienced something so powerful that it still affects my life to this day. With complete clarity I realized I was not alone in that desolate room. The veil of suffering lifted and I saw clearly a figure standing near me. He wore a white robe more vivid than any earthly garment I have ever seen. Though I could not make out his features, I could tell he was bearded. Then, in a voice I heard with my whole being, he told me, "Paul, you are going to be all right. I am always with you."

I was still bound but suddenly I felt free, the flames of my despair smothered by comfort and reassurance. Those words, I knew, were the words of Jesus, delivered by an angel. It was Christ alone who had command over life, and He was telling me that with Him all suffering could be endured, all pain soothed.

Suddenly my companion was no longer visible, and I was alone again with my pitiful meal. Yet it beckoned me like a feast. I tipped over the stool and ate gratefully.

I survived two more weeks of intermittent torture that particular go-around with the interrogators, and for four more years I was a captive in the Hanoi Hilton. In 1973 I was finally able to come home and get started on some of those business plans I had dreamed up in my prison cell to pass the long, solitary hours. That day when the angel delivered the words that saved me, I *did* make a confession—a confession of faith. My life was saved, not just once but forever.

A Touch on the Shoulder

by Haven Webster

Two winters ago my stepsister, Dana, came to live with us. She was my age, 15. Her dad is my stepdad, and he lives with Mom and me and my younger sister Heidi in a small town just south of Greensboro, North Carolina. Dana and her brother had lived with their mom in a nearby town. My stepsiblings had spent weekends with us for years, and I had always enjoyed having an extra brother and sister around to play with.

But when Dana hit adolescence, things changed. *Dana* changed. One night Dana's mother called and talked to my stepdad for an hour. Finally he got off the phone.

"Dana's having some problems," he said quietly. "And her mom wants to get her away from the crowd she's running with." My stepdad paused. "Can we pull together for Dana and have her come live with us for a while?"

Mom was eager. "Sure we can."

"Of course," said Heidi.

I got this knot in my stomach. The decision clearly affected my life most. She'd have to transfer to my school, my grade. I played on the girls' basketball team; my friends were not a wild bunch. Some were athletes, all of them studied hard, a lot of them went to church. We respected our parents and followed the rules. That wasn't Dana's way. Why should her problems now be dumped on us?

"Where's she going to sleep?" I asked, hoping to nix the idea. The three bedrooms in our home were already occupied. "She can't live on the couch, can she?" Mom and my stepdad looked disappointed.

"My bedroom's the biggest," said Heidi. "She can share it with me." And so it was settled.

Winter 1994 was the most unpleasant season in the history of our home. Dana brushed in angrily that first night and hardly spoke while Mom and Heidi fell all over themselves, helping her unpack and making her feel welcome. I hung back, watching, wondering when the big storm would come. I didn't have to wait long.

My stepdad poked his head in the bedroom door. "Let's all go for ice cream!"

"Count me out," Dana said. And she made it clear she wasn't interested in any of our goody-two-shoes activities. My stepdad made her come anyway, and we all climbed into the car, none of us with an appetite for ice cream.

Later, alone in my bedroom, I went down on my knees. "Dear Lord, help us get through this. Change Dana so we can go back to normal." But my resentment grew when I heard Mom's footsteps hurrying down toward Heidi and Dana's room to wish them a good night.

Several mornings later I noticed dark circles around Mom's eyes. Because of all the chaos, she wasn't getting enough rest. "This is totally unfair," I complained to her.

"Things will get better," Mom said patiently. "Dana needs us." Mom took every opportunity to give her a compliment or a hug. And I wondered, *How can Mom try so hard when Dana isn't trying at all?*

Dinner at our house became a tense scene. Everyone seemed to be on edge. Gone were the animated conversations. Heidi was her chatty self, but I was definitely quieter. Mom and my stepdad had enough to worry about without listening to my frivolous teenage concerns, like the new outfit I coveted or how hard practice had been.

One night after doing the dishes my stepdad and I went outside to shoot some baskets. While I had him alone, I thought I'd fill him in on what had been going on in *my life* since Dana's arrival. These days his focus always seemed to be on her. "I walk her to every class, I've introduced her to my friends, invited her to basketball games and to hang out. I've helped her with homework, explained school projects. What else am I supposed to do? What more does she want?"

My stepdad sighed. "I don't know, Haven," he said. "I just don't know." He bounced the ball. I wished I'd kept my mouth shut. Maybe my life wasn't affected most, after all.

For the first time I considered how Dana might be feeling. She'd moved into a new home, and switched in midyear to a new school. It couldn't have been easy. I'd gone through the motions with her, but personally I'd pretty much kept my distance. Maybe that wasn't right. "God," I asked at bedtime, "help me to be more sisterly toward Dana."

My nightly prayers slowly but surely became more sincere. But the days always seemed to bring more nightmares. Why wouldn't God simply work a miracle and change Dana instantly? She'd been living with us for four long months, and I saw no end to the "temporary" setup.

Then something strange happened. On a night early in April I was awakened from a sound sleep. I never wake up in the middle of the night. Never. Normally, a radio playing full blast couldn't wake me, but that night, at 1:00 A.M., something did. At the foot of my bed was an angel. He was clothed in pure white, with a bright light shining all around him. I couldn't see his face—it was surrounded by a sparkle—but when he spoke, his voice was deep, and urgent: "Tell her before it's too late."

"Tell who what?" I asked.

Reaching out toward me, he said again, "Tell her before it's too late."

I wasn't afraid, just completely puzzled. "Who?" I asked, mentally going down the list of my best friends' names. Who needed to hear something from me?

The deep-voiced angel simply repeated, "Tell her before it's too late." Then he was gone and my thoughts that night were full of questions. Why me?

I kept the angel's visit to myself. Who would believe me anyway? I wasn't even sure exactly what had happened—until two nights later.

He came back, this time even before I had fallen asleep. He

appeared right beside my headboard and tapped my shoulder to get my attention. His message was the same, but even more urgent. "Tell her."

"Who?"

"Dana."

And he was gone.

In algebra the next day, I stared at the *x*'s in the equations on the blackboard. What could I tell Dana? That I had been praying for God to change her radically and he was taking his time about it? Looking back, I had to admit she had made small efforts. She cheered at my basketball games, but I figured family was supposed to do that. She had pulled up her grades, though it was either that or be grounded. She was making friends of her own, including some pretty good kids, like Krystal, one of the cheerleaders. And at least she'd stopped bellyaching about going to church. Dana had even joined the choir, which Mom directed. Very un-Danalike. . . .

Now that I thought about it, things were much more pleasant at home. Dana *had* begun to change. I was the one who hadn't. I was as impatient as ever with God, and I suppose I was somewhat unwilling to share my parents' attention.

Maybe I needed to change some things about myself too.

That afternoon after school I did what I always did when I had a problem: I went to Mom. I told her about the angel's visits. "I know God loves me," I said. "And I love Dana. But I still don't know what to tell her."

"Tell her how you feel," Mom said simply. "Tell her about God's love. Here's your chance to help your sister."

That evening, I got my courage up. "Dana," I said, "there's something I've got to tell you. Will you come on back to my room?" Dana looked at me skeptically. In all the time she'd lived with us, I don't think I'd ever invited her into my private sanctuary.

We sat on my bed. I was tense, not knowing how or where to begin. So I looked her straight in the eye and told her everything, about seeing an angel, about being sisters, and about God's love and how powerful it is. How we can do anything when we know it is for real. "The angel came because God cares about us," I told her. "He loves us." I began to cry and Dana reached out and hugged me. "I really care what happens to you," I told her.

"I care about you too," she said.

I'd prayed for the change in Dana. But more important, God had changed me. I had asked him to touch one heart, and he took the opportunity to touch two.

A VOICE IN THE BLIZZARD

by Vance Thurston

Bitter cold had made life a struggle on the plains of northeastern Montana. Darkness was rapidly approaching and snow crunched beneath my insulated boots. I held my hand to my face, blocking the raw wind. Lady, my border collie, huddled close to my feet as she would when a storm was coming in. After another day spent coaxing frozen machinery to run and feeding cattle, I felt weary all over.

I thought about going straight home while there was still light. My own place was more than a mile south from the ranch where I worked. Since the road was blocked by eight-foot-high drifts, I had been traveling back and forth by snowmobile. But my wife Mary was working the night shift at the hospital and wouldn't be home for dinner. So when Charlie, one of the ranch owners, offered to cook, I decided to stay and eat with him.

After supper I trudged out to the shop to fix a broken weld on the loader tractor so it wouldn't hold us up in the morning. I didn't think it would take long, but nothing had gone right that day.

I lost track of time. Finally the increasing howl of the wind caught my attention. Concerned, I tried to open the shop door to look outside, but a drift was blocking it. I struggled to push the door open and a blast of snow hit me in the face. The ranch house was difficult to see even though it was only 150 feet away. The storm blocked any moonlight, and drifts made the short walk difficult. After reaching the house I scraped ice off the thermometer. It had already dropped to 28 below zero.

"Better stay here tonight," Charlie suggested. "You can sleep on the couch." But I felt compelled to go home and make sure the heat was working in our house. As I put on my winter gear, face mask and goggles, I told Charlie, "I'll follow the fence line home instead of cutting across the pasture." After all, I had spent more than 30 years in Montana; I could certainly handle bad weather. Lady held back as I urged her out the door into the heightening blizzard.

It was so cold that the track on the snowmobile was frozen. I finally got it started, and Lady dutifully climbed into her usual spot on the seat in front of me. I maneuvered around a large drift that covered a corner post. It took a minute to find the fence in the swirling blackness. Reassured, I worked my way along, reminding myself to stay as close to the fence as possible.

Out on the open plain the blizzard grew with frightening intensity. Snow swirled crazily in the headlight. I could no longer see the front runners. My goggles iced over and when I tried to clean them they filled with snow. Hunching closer to the windshield, I hugged the fence line.

Suddenly the snowmobile lurched. I fought for control as Lady scrambled on the seat. When I looked back, the fence line was gone.

"It's still there," I reassured myself. "I've just drifted to the right." Slowly I turned left. Nothing. I kept turning, expecting to bump into the fence at any moment. Making a fist in my leather mitt, I attempted to warm my numbing fingertips. I decided to travel in a slow circle, concentrating on keeping the snowmobile upright as I felt my way in the unknown darkness.

Nothing—except the moaning wind. I tried what I thought was a larger circle. I couldn't make sense of what was happening. Was this the first sign of hypothermia? The windchill was inescapable. I was freezing. How much time did I have?

Lady looked like an ice-covered porcupine. She stared at me with a bewildered expression as if to ask, "What are we doing?" I considered turning her loose to see if she could find the way home. But how would we be able to keep track of each other in this screaming hell of ice? I knew I could not expect rescue from Charlie because I had the only working snowmobile.

Hugging Lady for comfort, I forced my mind to reason. If only I could find the fence line. But how?

In desperation I said a rusty Sunday school prayer. That seemed to help me, so I got more personal. *Dear God,* I prayed, *I am in a heap of trouble. Please help me.* Slowly an idea began to form: *Use the snowmobile light for a beacon and search for the fence.*

Turning the light on high, I got off the snowmobile and started to push my way through the waist-deep snow. After a few steps the wind drowned out all sound of the running engine. If the engine died, the light would too. I forced myself forward as Lady stumbled in my tracks. I tried to carry her, but I didn't have the strength. We struggled on until the light was a dim glow behind us. Nothing. We turned around, drifts already burying our tracks.

When we got back, the snowmobile engine compartment was filling with snow so I turned the sled upwind and tried to speed the idle. When I squinted into the storm, snow collected on my eyelashes and froze my eyes shut. There was nothing to do but plunge forward in another direction. I forced them open and leaned against the wind. Where were we? Nothing made sense. There were miles of prairie and I could find no landmarks. Again we returned to the snowmobile.

The engine was barely running. How much longer could it last? Reluctantly we cast out again on foot. Glancing back at the fading light I fell face-forward. I lay there, snow covering my freezing body. I was so tired and defeated I just wanted to sleep.

I thought about Mary. I wanted to tell her how much I loved her. I thought about our daughter and wondered how she would grow up. *Dear God,* I prayed, *help me live!*

Lady nuzzled my face. I spit the snow out of my mouth and struggled to my feet. Then, above the roar of the storm, a voice seemed to say, "Just a little farther." Was I hearing things? The wind mocked me as if to answer, "Your mind is going." And yet the voice was so compelling that somehow I pushed myself forward. Again I fell, but this time I had tripped on something. Digging frantically I came up with a strand of barbed wire that led to a fence post hidden under the snow.

I nursed the snowmobile back to the wire and followed it. My pockets were filling with snow and I was losing hope when the wire rose out of the snow and became a visible fence. Still I wasn't sure. The wind was moving drifts, changing the landscape before my eyes. I groped on.

The fence had ended! A post with an old piece of rope flapping in the wind marked the end of the line. We seemed so close—but to what? Lady was staring in a distinct direction, her head slightly cocked. Was it the ranch? My teeth chattered, and fear seemed to swirl in the wind. But again I heard the voice: "Just a little farther." Was it my imagination?

I squeezed the throttle and the snowmobile went forward. Suddenly we pitched to a stop. I realized where we were. We had collided with the posts of the ranch-yard cattle guard. A moment later I could see the yard light swaying violently in the wind. We were going to make it!

Lady was mighty glad to be back at the ranch and so was I. Charlie thawed me out with a lot of coffee, but I didn't feel much like talking. I had been gone only two hours, but it had felt like an eternity. I went to bed and Lady slept close by me.

Later the next day, when the storm finally broke, I went outside to figure out how I had become so lost. My almost-fatal error seemed unbelievable in the light of day. While leaving the yard and swinging around the huge mound of snow, I had lost my sense of direction and started down the wrong fence line. That fence went out toward the horizon and disappeared into the endless drifts. I shuddered. How amazing it was that I had found that wire—my lifeline—under those mounds of snow! As I thought about the voice, I felt mighty grateful I was back at work and able to feed the cows that day.

Things have changed since then. The old fence has been torn down, and my dear dog Lady lies buried beside the creek. I still fall short at times, but I take comfort in knowing we are children of God, loved and cared for even in our darkest hours. I still remember my prayer in the blizzard and how much I wanted to live. When I remember the voice—*Just a little farther*—I feel at peace. I was hopelessly lost in a blizzard when the grace of God led me home.

A Memory of Glory

by John Sherrill

"I write these things...so that you may know that you have eternal life."
—I John 5:13 (NIV)

There is one aspect of aging that none of us likes to consider: the approaching end of life. Yet, because of one fragile experience, I shall never again look upon death in the same way.

At seven o'clock one dark October morning in 1993, I stepped into the side chapel of our church. Two days earlier I'd lost a close friend and prayer partner, Bob Nardozzi, and I'd come here to wrestle with my grief.

I turned on the light, sat down and began to read the Bible as I had often done in this special place. The chapel was a favorite of mine because of a splendid Tiffany window that depicts St. Christopher crossing a river with the Christ Child on his shoulder. Today, however, the window matched my mood. In the dim artificial light the scene was sullen and lifeless.

For perhaps twenty minutes I immersed myself in the wonderful assurances of eternal life contained in the Book of John. When I looked up, a transformation had taken place in the window before me. The sun had risen behind the glass, displaying its colors in dazzling light. Christopher's face, his hands, the robes he wore, the river through which he walked that had seemed so dark and threatening, all pulsed with shimmering light.

In that moment I glimpsed the end of life on this earth, Bob's and my own, too, with new eyes.

As long as I look upon death with my own feeble, man-generated lights, it appears bleak and forbidding. But when I see it in the light shining on it from the other side, then I see death from God's vantage point. Scripture provides that light. "For God so loved the world that he gave his one and only Son, that whoever believes in him shall not perish but have eternal life" (John 3:16, NIV).

Father, show me the passage we call death by the light of Your Word.

Cash Quest

by Brock Kidd

I really liked college, but one thing I missed was being able to raid the family refrigerator anytime I wanted.

I remember one time when my friend Rob and I had been studying for a huge test. We'd been up half the night, and we were starving.

"Got any money?" Rob asked. "I'm thinking pizza."

I went through my pockets. One dollar bill. Two quarters. I went over to the desk and rummaged through the drawer. Seven pennies. In the meantime, Rob had come up with another dollar and fifteen cents.

"Oh, man," I said, "I wish you hadn't mentioned pizza."

Well, now we were desperate to find the money. We could almost smell the pepperoni and cheese. We went to the living room of the fraternity house where we lived. We lifted the cushions on the couch and looked under all the furniture. Another nickel, a dime and another quarter.

"Hey, what about our coat pockets!" I said, heading back toward the room.

On the way, something told me to stop at the mail table in the hall. I was surprised to see a letter addressed to me in my sister Keri's handwriting. I ripped open the letter, and a ten dollar bill fluttered to the floor. "Have a pizza on your sister," I read in amazement. Keri was in the ninth grade at the time. I knew that this was money she had earned baby-sitting. Unbelievable that she would send it to me!

Before the hour was over, Rob and I were eating the best pizza of our lives.

The Bible says that if you delight in Him, God will give you "the desires of your heart" (Psalm 37:4). Now, I'm pretty sure that Psalmist wasn't talking about pepperoni pizza. But I'm certain that on that night, God showed His love to two tired college kids by sending them what they wanted most. And it came in a big square box from the local pizzeria.

7 Working Relationships

Do all the good you can,
By all means you can,
In all the ways you can,
In all the places you can,
At all the times you can,
To all the people you can,
As long as ever you can.

— John Wesley

Five-fingered Fred

by Melinda Champlin

Too late. I saw the empty bucket roll out from underneath the shelf just as my foot caught the handle. I landed with a crash. The stack of ceramic bowls I had been carrying clattered to the floor, smashing with a clang that echoed throughout the kitchen. As I brushed the broken pieces from my apron, my boss hurried in, his scowl lost within his sagging cheeks.

"What do you think you're doing?" he bellowed.

"Making a mosaic," I replied, attempting humor.

"Do you know how much bowls cost?" His bulldog face shook angrily.

My eyes widened. "Fred," I said, struggling to be patient, "I have no idea how much bowls cost and I'm sorry I broke them, but shouldn't you have *first* asked if I was hurt?"

But he hadn't heard me—he was already out of the kitchen, doors swinging behind him. I struggled to my feet in frustration and anger. As I gathered the scattered pieces, my emotions cooled and I began to contemplate.

I was 17 years old and experiencing the most incredible summer of my life. Weeks earlier I had left Massachusetts and embarked on the two-day journey that landed me in southeast Alaska, the place my grandparents have called home for the past 50 years. I was thrilled by the constant adventure: living in a log cabin; bear-watching; kayaking; flying on sea planes. The only thing I didn't like were the outhouses. But I would have preferred an eternity of smelly outhouses to Fred, head chef at the fishing lodge where I waitressed.

The first thing I noticed about Fred was that he only smiled if the customers were watching; otherwise he stomped around, his tired face set into a frown.

The next thing I noticed about Fred was that he didn't like me. His dislike was partly my fault; we didn't exactly get off to a great start. Upon meeting him I had asked what time I should be at work the next morning. He held up his hand as if to display five fingers—only Fred doesn't have five fingers on any one hand. The hand he held up had three fingers and two stubs. During his many years as a chef, several of his fingers had fallen victim to his kitchen knives.

I didn't want to offend Fred, but I was confused. Was I supposed to count each missing finger as one? Or did he expect me not to count them at all? Or maybe I was supposed to count each stub as a half. *He knows they're missing,* I thought. I bit my lip and took a chance.

"You need me at four?"

His eyes narrowed into slits as he shook his head, and continued to hold up his hand. By now the whole staff was listening.

"Fred," I pleaded, "Please just say it. I . . . um, I don't see very well without my glasses." A staff member stifled a giggle. Desperate, I tried again.

"Five?"

He nodded and stormed out, the crew's laughter following him into the kitchen.

From that point on I had an enemy. If I said "good morning" to a guest, I was yelled at for socializing on work time. When I excused myself from a conversation with a talkative patron, Fred screamed at me for being rude.

Despite Fred's attacks, I tried to treat him with kindness and respect. But as the days wore on my tolerance wore out, and I began to fight back. I felt that if I didn't, I would be leaving my self-esteem at the mercy of Fred. Every time Fred hollered at me,

I hollered back, matching him volume for volume, insult for insult.

As the days dragged by, the situation worsened, and for some reason my self-esteem didn't improve.

Retreating from these thoughts, I knelt to retrieve the last of the broken bowls. Just then Fred scurried by, pausing for a moment to frown, his face reflected in the glossy whiteness of my ceramic pile. As I gazed at his reflection I was filled with a sudden sadness. I knew God loved Fred just as much as he loved me. So why couldn't I love Fred as much as I loved the Lord?

Shame slowly settled over me. I had convinced myself I had done everything possible to get along with Fred. But had I really?

Then I did what I should have done in the beginning: I turned my problem over to the Lord. As I knelt there on the floor I said a prayer for Fred. It was the first of many.

Praying for Fred wasn't easy. Why should I pray for him when he was so awful? He was ruining what *could* have been the perfect summer job. But I knew the Lord had the power to help Fred change. So I prayed for Fred in the mornings, and I prayed for Fred in the evenings. And when Fred unjustly criticized me, I prayed even harder.

Then one day it happened. Fred pulled me aside for what I assumed was more criticism. But he looked at his shuffling feet and muttered, "Ya know . . . back when I was a teenager I didn't play loud music or go out with friends. Why, when I was fourteen, I went to work. And it wasn't easy work either—this was hard manual labor . . . so you see, I haven't got the ability to understand you teenagers. I know I've been harsh with you, and I want you to know I don't mean it."

My mind reeled. I couldn't believe it—Fred was apologizing!

After that, I forgot how much I hated his cooking, or his unsettling habit of simultaneously popping sausages and heart medication into his mouth. I started noticing nice things about Fred, like how he loved to cook the staff special foods.

I didn't mind so much when he yelled. I guess you could even say I was starting to like Fred. We started having real conversations as we sat in the kitchen waiting for things to cook. We talked about religion and God, and who had caught the biggest fish. He taught me how to tell when a pancake is cooked completely through, and how to crack 50 eggs in less than 20 seconds.

At the close of the season I returned home with more than a box of frozen Alaskan fish. Five-fingered Fred had taught me that despite a person's faults—my own included—God loves everyone unconditionally, and with prayer and faith we can do the same.

BEGGAR FOR THE POOR

by Ferdinand Mahfood

My father was a dry-goods merchant in Kingston, Jamaica, and from the time I was seven years old I performed an important task at his store. On Fridays, whenever I wasn't in school, I gave money to the poor.

Early in the morning when the bank opened, I stood in line, clutching the five-pound note my father had given to me. The teller greeted me with familiarity and counted out the pennies carefully before I put them in my pocket. By the time I returned to 136 Harbor Street, beggars were standing in a long line that stretched past the painted, green and white sign that read, "Mahfood's Commercial Ltd.," past the steel shutters and down around the corner.

One by one beggars held out their hands. "Thank you, master," they said as I put the pennies in their palms. In those days in Jamaica a penny went a long way. Sometimes I wondered who these poor people were and how they spent their money. But most of the time my interest never went further than the shiny pennies that were gobbled up by the hungry hands.

As I grew older, Father gave me other tasks at the store. A Lebanese immigrant, he had landed in Jamaica as a young man with barely a cent to his name. After working in a store, he started his own wholesale business and built it into one of the largest in the country. He supplied hundreds of retail outlets throughout Jamaica with hats, shoes, suits, trousers, linen, lace, braids and yarn. He had an uncanny knack for knowing what people wanted and a gift for striking a bargain. "Remember, son," he told me, "buying carefully is everything. That's where the money is."

In 1956, when I was 18 years old, he sent me on my first buying trip to Manchester, England. I had a specific list and a tight budget. With it I had to buy gabardine for suits, wool flannel, horsehair lining, stiffening fabric for collars and a certain hat that was all the rage back home. I took my list from one vendor to another and, using every skill I had acquired, I bought carefully, coming home with 35,000 English pounds' worth of merchandise. My father was a stern disciplinarian and I knew he would be displeased if I had spent a penny too much. To my delight he congratulated me when I returned. I had learned my lesson and had bargained well.

After my father's death I took over the business with my four younger brothers. We expanded into an import-export company and profited handsomely, buying carefully and selling well. My wife Patti and I built our home on a palm-tree-shaded hill outside Kingston. I bought a yacht, put in a swimming pool and a tennis court. With our three children we lived a comfortable, prosperous life. And like my father, I came up with a project for giving to the poor.

I regularly rented Hollywood films for my children and showed them at home with our own projector. Then one day on a church retreat I was inspired to take these movie nights to orphanages and hospitals. I found a distributor to provide the latest movies, another to give me boxes of candy and a third who supplied comic books. Once a month I visited the underprivileged and entertained them. It became a quaint tradition, like handing out pennies on Friday at Mahfood's Commercial Ltd. I suppose I stopped myself from thinking any deeper about the poor and their lives.

In the 1970s Patti and I moved to Florida, where my brothers and I continued our flourishing business. One Christmas, Patti gave me a volume by the writer Catherine Marshall. I figured I would look into the book when I was on a business trip. I dropped it into my briefcase and thought nothing more of it.

Two weeks later, on a bitterly cold January day, when I was flying to Chicago for a convention, I opened the book. I read what Catherine Marshall wrote about the Holy Spirit. She was talking about how the Spirit, or the Comforter, as she called him, wrapped her in an overwhelming love after the death of her husband. At once I was overcome. At that moment, in a way I can never fully explain, I felt surrounded and filled by God's love. I had always called myself a believer, but this was an awareness of God, of divine presence, that I had never before experienced. I wasn't sure what was happening to me, but I knew it was beyond my ability to control it.

Lord, I prayed after savoring the feeling, *what do You want of me?* I was ready to do anything I could for God. The answer came to me as if he had spoken it: *Give me yourself.*

The next few years were an exciting time of spiritual growth. I began to pray every day. Early in the morning, before work began and before the phones started ringing, I went into an empty room in my house and read the Bible, then closed my eyes, listening carefully for God's word in my life. *How,* I asked, *can I give myself to You?*

First I did the obvious thing: I gave money to people and organizations that were helping the poor. Soon my staff and I were assisting seven or eight programs. But I still wondered if there was something more I could do.

On a trip back to Jamaica in 1981, a missionary took me to visit a poorhouse called Eventide. We drove down a narrow, dusty street, the gutter an open sewer. Families dug through garbage in search of their next meal. Children with twisted legs and young men with leprosy begged piteously when they saw our car pass. Inside the poorhouse were hundreds of men, women and children. Barely clothed, they sat on the floor staring into space, flies buzzing around them as if they were refuse. Some were so thin I wondered how they were able to breathe. And yet I had seen these faces before. They were the faces outside my father's store so many years ago. Now I knew: These were the faces of Christ.

On that trip it all became clear. My gifts as a businessman were perfect for a huge job that needed to be done. Running a large import-export firm, I had acquired the management skills to ship merchandise throughout the Caribbean. I knew how to cut governmental red tape. And I knew how to bargain to get the best merchandise for the best price. Missionaries had built facilities like this one for the poor. What they needed were supplies. That I could provide.

Since then the organization I started, Food For The Poor, has provided more than 250 million dollars in aid to Jamaica, Haiti, Guyana, Grenada and several countries in Latin America. I follow our donations to their destinations, making sure resources are used wisely. Like my father quizzing his customers, I ask people what they need. Then I go out and get it at the best price I can.

On a recent visit to Haiti I asked the nun in charge of the Mother Teresa Home for the Dying what she needed.

"Sheets," she said.

"How many?" I asked.

"Three hundred."

I wrote the figure down. "Done," I said, as I added to my list. It wasn't all that different from my first trip to England. I think my father would be proud of how I do business today. Whether I'm buying medicine, grain, school desks, sewing machines, disinfectant or hundreds of bedsheets, I bargain down to my last penny. These are the skills I have acquired and the lessons I've learned. But these days I bargain for Jesus. I do it for the poor. What we are dealing in is love. And that is the most precious commodity.

Down, But Not Out

by Stuart Levine and Michael Crom

Contrary to what most people believe, outside influences do not usually determine personal happiness and success. What matters is how we react to those influences, good or bad.

Marshall and Maureen Cogan achieved great success. He was a partner at a big New York investment-banking firm. She was a rising star in the publishing business. The Cogans owned a beautiful co-op apartment in the city, and they had just built an expensive summer home near the ocean in East Hampton. The three Cogan children seemed to love that house as much as their parents did.

Then Marshall decided to strike out on his own. Despite his high expectations, the new business never got off the ground. Marshall sank all his savings into the business, and almost overnight it was worthless. This bad luck was topped off by one final blow: At the most crucial point of his struggles to keep the business afloat, Marshall came down with hepatitis, which confined him to bed for more than a month.

Marshall's bankers demanded he sell the new house. So the Cogans sold their house, along with every piece of furniture.

"We should take the kids out to the house," Maureen told

Marshall the day before the new owners were set to arrive. "We can give each one of them a big trash bag to put their toys in, and we can bring all that stuff back to the city."

Marshall disagreed: "I don't want them to be a part of this."

"No way," Maureen told him. "They're going to understand what it is to be down, because they're going to watch you come back. And they're going to understand that if that happens to them one day, they, too, can come back."

So everyone rode out to East Hampton. The children cleaned out their rooms, while the parents collected their personal effects. Then the five of them climbed back in the car for the drive to the city. That's when Maureen spoke quietly to Marshall: "Life will go on."

And then she talked to the kids. "No, we don't have our house," she said. "But we have a nice apartment. We're together. Daddy's healthy, and he's going to start a new business. Everything's going to be fine."

Soon enough, Marshall was back in business and doing well. More important, a lesson had been learned, a lesson that showed up almost 20 years later.

Explains Maureen: "Our oldest son started a business that we had to close down so it would not go bankrupt. It was a tough failure for him, and he was young, just twenty-five. I remember him saying, 'It's awful. I've got a few more months before I'm closed.'

"But then he said, 'I remember when it happened to Daddy, and I'll be fine. I will get through this, because I watched, and I remember.'"

How do you develop that kind of outlook? How do you control your reactions to outer forces? By making it a conscious priority.

"When you put your feet on the floor in the morning," explains Stanley R. Welty, Jr., president of the Wooster Brush Company, "you'll make it a good day or a bad day by controlling your thought processes. We're either going to enjoy life that day or we're not."

After years of struggle, things were finally looking up for Mary Kay Ash. She had remarried. The children were finally grown. She and her new husband had saved just enough money to start a small cosmetics company, a dream she had nurtured for years.

Then her dream nearly disintegrated. "The day before we were to open this company," Ash recalls, "my husband died of a heart attack at the breakfast table. He was to handle the administration of the company. I don't know a thing about administration, even today.

"On the day of the funeral, my two sons and my daughter and I sat down to decide what to do. Do I stop or go on?"

Mary Kay Ash believed in herself too much to give up. Her son Richard, who was just 20, offered to do what he could. "Mother," he said, "I'll move to Dallas to help."

Ash had her doubts, but didn't let doubt overwhelm her. She pressed on. "That was the beginning of the company. True to his word, Richard and his wife moved to Dallas the next day. The lawyers were saying, 'Why don't you go directly to the trash and throw the money in, because you're never going to make it.'"

Her positive attitude got her through it all. She just kept telling herself, "I think it can be done, and I'm going to try." Is it any surprise that Ash and Mary Kay Cosmetics succeeded?

As Marshall Cogan and Mary Kay Ash demonstrate, the secret to building a happy life and a successful career is a positive attitude.

SIGNS OF THE TIMES

by Joe Friedman

During the Depression my father owned a grocery store in St. Joseph, Missouri, near the river. Back then the area was a stopping point for unemployed men crossing the country looking for jobs. Sometimes they worked for food or a place to stay, but generous folk often gave them a handout.

As they drifted from city to city or farm to farm, these tramps left secret codes scratched onto fences or barns. Chalk marks designated where a meal or a good night's sleep awaited a hungry, weary traveler. For example, a happy face indicated a barn you could sleep in. Other symbols showed where a man could get help when sick, or warned of bad drinking water. And no one would barter work at a home with the mark of a saber, the sign of a dishonest man.

Times were hard for us too. Dad, an immigrant from Russia, had first worked as an itinerant peddler, selling thread, needles and dry goods. When he bought the store he often struggled to keep it fully stocked. Dad had shown me how to move the groceries and cans to the front of the shelves so it looked like we had more than we did. Even with five children to feed, he didn't hesitate to take in an orphaned nephew or extend credit. He prayed regularly and read the

Scriptures. True to them, he never turned a hungry person away.

When the train stopped in our town, the hoboes and tramps jumped the tracks and fanned up the street toward our grocery store, which was just 13 blocks from the railroad yard. On summer days Mother sat in front of the store with a pitcher of lemonade to refresh passersby. Inside, Dad kept a large tin of peanut butter and sliced bread on the counter to make sandwiches. Or he asked, "Would you like a slice of bologna and a half-pint of milk?" Sometimes they got both.

One day a rumpled old man with callused hands sauntered up to the meat case, wiping his brow with a ragged handkerchief. So many men with lean, lanky frames and patched overalls flooded the store that day that Dad asked the old man if he knew why.

"Come outside," said the old man. "I want to show you something." Curious, I tagged along. We walked around to the corner of the building, where the stone foundation met the street. There, scratched with a piece of coal, was the sign of the cross.

"What does this mean?" Dad asked in his accented English.

"That a good Christian man lives here. He will never turn away anyone asking for food."

My father smiled wryly and the three of us walked back into the store. Throughout those rough Depression years, Dad never erased that sign or fell short of what it advertised. A devout Orthodox Jew, he had come to this country to escape persecution. And he had learned that a good man could be found under more than one sign.

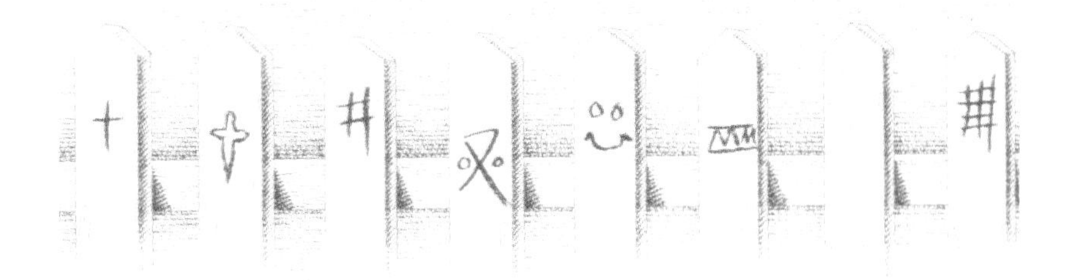

Something of Myself

by Ruth Stafford Peale

The thing I remember most vividly about that first job of mine was the department store customer who gave me such a hard time. She was a sharp-faced woman with a harsh voice, and I can see her now as she pawed through my neatly arranged merchandise at the ribbon counter, complaining, grumbling, criticizing, finding nothing that pleased her—and being quite rude in the process.

When I applied for that summer job, I had been told that, as far as salespeople were concerned, the customer was always right. It was hard to believe that such an impossible person as this could be right about anything. But I held my tongue. I needed the job, even if it paid only $11 a week.

When the difficult customer finally moved on after a small purchase, I drew a sigh of relief. As I began sorting my tangled merchandise, I reviewed my performance and even felt a little smug. I had remained calm and polite. I had kept smiling—most of the time, anyway. And after all, I told myself, such people were the exception, not the rule.

I had gotten the job on my own, partly to earn a little spending money, partly to help out at home. My father, a minister, was a man of great kindliness and dignity, but I doubt if he ever earned more than $2400 a year in his life. My mother, tiny and deeply devout, had a marked musical gift. She played the piano and sometimes gave music lessons that brought in a little extra cash. Both my brothers had paper routes. When one of them was sick, Mother and I would get up at five in the morning and walk the route, sometimes in freezing rain or deep snow. I didn't enjoy being a substitute papercarrier. But delivering the papers was a family responsibility, and in our family that concept was never taken lightly.

My father, who had a strong sense of justice, thought that $11 a week was very little for the store to be paying me, even if I was only 14 years old. He had advised me to ask for a raise, and (full of qualms) I had done so. At closing time that day, the manager called me in and told me that my request was granted. Henceforth, I would be paid $13 a week. "And do you know why?" he said. "We sent one of our shoppers to your counter this morning, a lady we use to check on the performance of our salespeople. We told her to be as difficult as possible—and to observe how you reacted. You passed the test very well indeed."

I don't think my feet touched the ground all the way home. I rushed in and threw my arms around my mother. "I got it! I got it!" When I told it again at the supper table, my father smiled. "You see," he said, "it pays to be patient and kind, no matter how unfair life may seem to be at the time."

It was a lesson far more valuable than the extra two dollars.

I was born in Fonda, Iowa, the second child in the family, and the only girl. My brother Charles—Chuck, we called him—was three years older. Two years after I was born, my brother Bill came along, and the family was complete.

All through my formative years, the sense of family solidarity and security was strong. We children didn't have many material possessions, but we had the peace of mind and the room to grow that come from a balanced combination of love and discipline inside the home. We had a lot of fun with music. Some of Mother's talent was passed along to all of us, and we spent a lot of time around the piano, harmonizing favorite songs and hymns.

Religion was an important part of our life, but it was not an ultrapious religion. It was something to be lived, not talked about. We said grace at meals. Sunday was a quiet day—no movies, no noisy games. From the start, my own faith seemed natural as breathing. I never had any intellectual doubts to resolve or great internal conflicts. I simply believed the Christian story and message, and drew strength when I needed it from my prayers and my faith.

Life was simpler for children in those days. Home was a place where honesty and decency were taught by example, not by decree. School was a place where good behavior was expected, where patriotism was encouraged, where diligence was rewarded.

I graduated from Northwestern High School at the age of 16 and had one year as a freshman at City College in Detroit where tuition was free; all a student had to pay for was books. But then a family dilemma arose. My brother Chuck was at Syracuse University with his senior year coming up. Family finances were strained to the utmost. If Chuck was to get his degree—and everyone agreed that he should—some sacrifices would have to be made. At a family conference, a decision was reached: I would drop out of college for a year and go to work to help Chuck complete his education. Then, when he had graduated and landed a job, he would repay me by helping me through three more years of college.

I must say, I was not too happy about this solution. I was only 17; I was enjoying myself at City College; I knew that all my friends and classmates would move on without me. But I accepted the plan with as much grace as I could muster, and went to work in the commercial department of the Michigan Bell Telephone Company in Detroit.

I worked there for a little more than a year. The responsibilities of a job made me mature much faster and showed me the advantages of a college education. When I did resume my studies, it was with my proper age group and I went to Syracuse University.

I majored in mathematics. I loved the sense that my mind was being trained in systematic thinking and logic. In my junior year, I moved into the Alpha Phi sorority house and had four roommates who shared a study-sitting room. It was there that I first heard about Norman Vincent Peale.

Girls at the sorority house who went to Norman's church on Sundays came back sighing romantically about the handsome young minister—miraculously unmarried at the age of twenty-nine—who held his congregation spellbound with sermons so eloquent and enthusiastic that going to church became an adventure, not an obligation. Sometimes, waves of laughter swept over the congregation in the great nave of the stately University Church. Evidently, he had a great sense of humor. Outside the church, he was said to be friendly, sociable and easygoing. But when he stood up in the pulpit, there was also an aura of great spiritual authority about him.

"You really ought to meet him, Ruth," my roommate Phyllis Leonard kept saying. "Or at least come to hear him preach. He's from the Midwest, like you—Ohio, I think. I know you'd like him."

It may be fanciful, but I believe that something in me even then was dimly aware that my destiny was linked with this unseen young man that all the girls were talking about. One night, Phyllis asked me to go with her to a party being given by the young people's group at the University Church. Just to stop her from harping on the subject any longer, I went.

It was a joyful evening with lots of interesting young people. Phyllis and I were about to leave when she said, "Ruth, you haven't even met Norman Peale. Come on, I will introduce you."

We went across the room and Phyllis said, "Mr. Peale, this is my roommate, Ruth Stafford."

We shook hands. And then a surprising thing happened. He held my hand just a fraction of a second longer than was necessary! I thought to myself, This is going to be interesting!

And it was. He was a bit embarrassed at calling a college girl, but he did so quite frequently. He said there were committees on which he wanted me to serve, especially one planning a big banquet for all the college people, with the famous Ralph Sockman from New York as the speaker. Would I be chairman of the committee?

One evening, he asked me to help him arrange the seating at the head table. We worked for quite a while and finally had everyone placed except for two empty seats together. "Who are these for?" I wanted to know. "Well," said Norman, "isn't it amazing? They must be for us!" And so they were.

More and more, I became aware that he was using me as a sounding board—testing ideas, trying out possible themes for sermons, seeking my reaction. He could be quite self-centered about this at times. I remember one trip to Cazenovia, where he was to give a talk that he called "Imprisoned Splendor," all about the shining potentials locked up inside all of us. He told me about it on the way to Cazenovia. He told me again as we had lunch at the old Linklaen House. He gave his talk and it went very well. Then, on the way home, he again suggested I drive. And while I battled the traffic, he told me all about "Imprisoned Splendor" for the fourth time!

But I didn't mind. When I saw how stirred his audiences were, and how people hearing him were uplifted and encouraged, I felt that it was a privilege to be a part—any part—of the creative process that made such eloquence and effectiveness possible.

As our friendship deepened, though, I began to realize that Norman's eloquence and creativity carried a price tag, and that price tag was a constant vulnerability to self-doubt, a hypersensitivity to any negative consideration where his work was concerned. Once, in the early days of our courtship, he asked me to tell him frankly what I thought of one of his sermons. So I told him frankly that in my opinion, while the beginning was effective, it sagged off a bit at the end. His reaction was one of complete despair. Overwhelmed with gloom, he told me that I had confirmed what he had long suspected: that he'd never be an effective preacher. He was clearly in the wrong profession. Perhaps he should get out of the ministry before it was too late.

Startled and dismayed, I struggled to correct my blunder . . . and finally succeeded. But I had learned a lesson that I have had to live with ever since: The highly creative person does not want objective criticism even when he thinks he does, or when he asks for it. He wants reassurance. He needs help and support in the endless, exhausting battle that he fights with his own merciless perfectionism.

I know that it all sounds a bit laughable, and Norman and I have laughed over it many times. But if, as a somewhat naive college coed, I had failed to learn that lesson quickly and completely and finally, I doubt if we ever would have been married.

Another thing I had to learn (and I truly think God gave me the wisdom, because in those days I had little of my own) was that whatever Norman's basic characteristics were, they were not going to change. He was a grown man, 29 years old, with his character fully formed, all its great gifts and talents and potentials established, but all its defects, too. If I were going to love him (and I was falling as deeply and rapidly in love as a girl ever did), if I were going to share his life and bear his children and help him reach out and transform lives, I was going to have to take him as he was and adapt my own personality to his.

And there was only one way to do this: Study the man. Learn everything about him. Learn to know him better than he knew himself. Learn to analyze his needs as coolly as if they were problems in mathematics that needed solutions. Learn what sort of fuel his personality required for maximum performance, find the right mixture, and supply it.

Our romance progressed swiftly. Too swiftly, I think, for Norman's mother. She came at his invitation to hear him preach the Mother's Day sermon in the University Church. I was impressed. It was clear that much of Norman's gift with words, much of his imagination, much of the romantic element in his makeup came from her.

Unfortunately, Mother Peale was not equally impressed with me. She had great plans, great dreams for Norman. She had accepted the restrictions of life as a small-town minister's wife herself, but she believed her oldest boy had the seeds of greatness in him. She was not unconscious of the value of wealth and social position—and when she looked at me, she could see neither in my family background. She was friendly and polite, but also a bit distant. She didn't directly try to discourage Norman, but she made it clear that if we became engaged she hoped it would be a long engagement. Very long.

It was. After I graduated, Norman helped me find a teaching job. I taught mathematics at Central High School in Syracuse at a salary of $1800 a year (Norman was making a princely $5500). All around us, the country seemed to be riding a dizzy wave of prosperity as the "Roaring Twenties" drew to a close. But I had to count my pennies carefully.

Two years after I had graduated from Syracuse, Norman and I were married in the University Church in Syracuse on a blue and gold June day. I knew as we walked out of the church together that a great adventure was beginning for both of us.

Now, after all these years, I still marvel at what a rich and rewarding pilgrimage it has been.

AILEEN AND ME

by Edward Grinnan

But I have called you friends....
—John 15:15

There is a woman whom I follow everywhere in New York. Her name is Aileen, and she cuts my hair. I first encountered Aileen when she worked at the salon in Bloomingdale's, and I had a half-price coupon for hair-styling. I liked what she did with my obstreperous locks—somehow she got them to behave. So, when Aileen moved from Bloomingdale's to a little shop on East 58th Street, I loyally followed. When she left that job without another to go to, she came by my apartment and cut my hair over the kitchen sink. Later, she was hired by what I was told was the trendiest salon in Manhattan, where patrons booked weeks in advance and paid a pretty price for the privilege. Aileen and I didn't feel comfortable there. We moved on.

Aileen was quite young when we started, and I was, well, younger. She lived an exuberant nightlife back then, sometimes showing up for her first appointment without having gone to bed. I saw her meet the man of her dreams, get married and join a venerable old Dutch Reformed Church in the East Village. Her work area used to be covered by postcards from downtown art galleries and dance clubs. Now she keeps pictures of her young son and his grandmas.

We're settled in now, the two of us, at another department store salon. It's funny to think I've known Aileen longer than I've known my wife or been at my job. My hair is starting to show just a touch of gray. I've never socialized with Aileen outside of her work and I've never seen her without a pair of clippers in her hand, but yesterday while she was finishing up by disciplining my cowlick with some hair gel, she said, "You know, you've changed." I thought she was going to tell me my hairline had eroded some since last visit, but no. "You're mellower," she said.

I don't quite know what that means, "mellower." But I've been thinking it over and the next time I see this woman—not exactly a friend but certainly not a stranger, I have something to tell her: We've mellowed together.

I am thankful, God, not just for the people You bring into my life but for those whom You keep there as we journey on Your path.

Worth Working For

by Aline A. Newman

When Iqbal Masih, a 12-year-old boy from Pakistan, visited Broad Meadows Middle School in Quincy, Massachusetts, the first thing the kids noticed was his size. "He looked like he was 6," recalls Amy Papile.

But there was nothing small about the message Iqbal brought: kids should have the right to go to school.

The *right*?

Iqbal had only recently gotten the chance to go to school himself. That's because when he was 4 years old, his father "sold" him to a carpet maker for $12. The carpet maker locked Iqbal in a dark shed. For fourteen hours a day, the little boy squatted before a carpet loom, tying knots in yarn. Sometimes he was chained to his loom. If he was bad or slow or cried for his mother, the carpet master beat him.

"Iqbal had a scar on his forehead from being beaten with a carpet tool," says Amy.

When Iqbal was 10, he escaped from the factory. Human rights workers placed him in a school where he learned quickly. Then they helped Iqbal begin campaigning against child labor. He won awards for bravery, but also made many enemies.

Four months after visiting Broad Meadows, Iqbal was shot near his grandmother's house in Pakistan. His murder has never been solved.

"I started building up this huge anger," says eighth-grader Amanda Loos.

But she turned anger to action when she and her classmates at Broad Meadows decided to build a school outside Iqbal's hometown in Kasir, Pakistan. "Education is power," says Amanda. "Without it, children will stay poor forever."

So she and her classmates wrote hundreds of letters and E-mail messages requesting donations. People from all 50 states and 12 foreign countries responded—and the students raised $106,700!

Now the new school is underway.

Why would any parent sell his own kid?

According to Pharis Harvey, Executive Director of the International Labor Rights Fund, "The family may be on the edge of starvation. They believe their child will be better off, because he will learn a trade and have food to eat."

That rarely happens.

Kids do boring jobs, like sewing soccer balls, weaving carpets or molding bricks. And masters keep them hungry on purpose, so they'll stay awake. These kids are forced to work because they're little and scared and easy to boss around.

The children earn only pennies a day. Out of this, the master takes a share for food, tools and mistakes. Most of what's left goes to the kids' parents and not to them. Consequently, few kids manage to buy back their freedom. Accidents kill some. Poor nutrition leaves survivors sickly and stunts their growth.

How big is this problem?

All this happens despite the fact that countries have laws against it. In fact, child slavery is a small part of a much larger problem: child labor. In Africa, Asia and Latin America, millions of kids toil long hours in unhealthy or dangerous conditions. They work on farms, as household servants or selling stuff on the street.

These kids aren't allowed to go to school or play with friends. They get little time off and hardly any pay. Their parents think working is more important than learning. They say work keeps kids busy and puts food in their bellies. So, what's the answer? Changing attitudes, better law enforcement and education help. One solution is to let kids work part-time, after classes.

What can *you* do?

"Take a closer look at things," suggests Amy. A "smiling carpet" label on a rug means it was made without child labor, for example. And of course you can write someone. "I wrote to the Prime Minister of Pakistan and to President Clinton," says Kevin Piccuito, 13.

Efforts like this pay off. Companies that make clothes in Pakistan just signed an agreement not to hire kids under 14 years old. This year, 7,000 kids will be in school instead of factories.

One of the most important things you can do is pray. "When you get the chance, stop and think," suggests Richard Keefe, 14. "Turn off the TV and pray for the children of Pakistan."

After all, Jesus *does* love all the children of the world.

If your computer is on-line, type this World Wide Web address:

http://www.digitalrag.com/iqbal/index.html

Broad Meadows Middle School will post regular updates as carpenters build the new school in Pakistan.

8

Loving Kids

Lord Jesus, You who bade the children come
And took them in Your gentle arms and smiled.
Grant me unfailing patience through the days
To understand and help my little child.

— Adelaide Love

"Lord, Keep My Kids Safe"

by Mae Bertha Carter

I woke up that September morning so filled with fear I could barely get out of bed. Matthew, my husband, was already up. He had fetched water from the pump, heated it up on the stove, and was filling the tub in the bedroom. Our five older children washed and got dressed while Matthew bathed our two youngest girls. I cooked breakfast. The kids were unusually quiet, no one talking excitedly about the first day of school. But then, school usually started for them in November, after most of the cotton had been picked.

Out of a wadded handkerchief I took seven quarters for lunch money and gave one to each of them—Deborah, Beverly, Pearl, Gloria, Stanley, Larry and Ruth. Then we waited on the front porch for the school bus.

Normally they would have been out in the cotton fields working. We worked from "can to can't," sunrise to sunset. Other families stopped picking on Fridays at noon. Not us Carters. We worked right through the weekend until Saturday night: four bales a week. Even after school, if there was any cotton left, the children picked. But I had decided I didn't want them stuck in a sharecropper's life.

I finally spotted the school bus coming our way. Not a rusty old hand-me-down, but a brand-new, yellow school bus. It stopped in front of our house. My kids were the first on. How would the other children react when they saw them there?

The fear came over me again. I watched the bus disappear down the road, then I went inside and lay across our bed. *Lord,* I prayed, *take care of my kids. Take care of my kids. Take care of my kids.* There have been times when I have felt God's covering, when I've sensed a protective peace all around. That was not one of them. My children had gone off to school. The only black children to enter a white school in Drew, Mississippi.

In 1965 the local school board—under court order—instituted something called freedom of choice. That summer, when the cotton wasn't open yet, and the only work we had to do was tend our own vegetable garden, I was off visiting relatives in St. Louis the day the choice notices arrived at the farm. My girl Ruth opened the letter and made up her mind right away. She wanted to go to the white school. She talked to the other kids and one by one they came to the same decision. All Matthew and I could say was, "If you want to go, we want you to go."

Early on August 12, Matthew and I put on our best clothes, climbed into our pickup and drove the nine miles into Drew. The town was quiet, but I felt as if everyone were peeking out of their windows at us. We stopped at the white high school, which was clean and freshly painted. It was the first time I had ever been inside. A secretary showed us into the principal's office. When we handed him the papers he got all red and flustered, but didn't say anything. We had no idea we were the only black parents in the county who had chosen to desegregate a school.

Word got out. The next day the plantation overseer, Mr. Thornton, drove up. "It's starting," Matthew muttered as he headed outside. I overheard Mr. Thornton telling my husband our kids could get a better education at the black school, and the white kids wouldn't talk to them, and black folks wouldn't have anything to do with us either.

I got so riled up I went inside, picked up a portable record player and a record my oldest son had given me of a President Kennedy speech about civil rights. I set the player on a chair near the door and turned the volume up so Mr. Thornton could hear Mr. Kennedy saying, "We are confronted primarily with a moral issue. It is as old as the Scriptures and is as clear as the American Constitution." We would not back down.

A few nights later Matthew was awakened at 3:00 A.M. by the sound of crunching gravel. He looked out the front window. "What on earth?" he muttered. The next thing I knew I was jolted out of bed by the pop-pop-pop of gunfire. *Lord, have mercy.* Bullets flew across the porch, shattering the windows. Bullets hit the wall above the bed where two of the kids were asleep. Scrambling through the house, Matthew and I brought all the kids to the back room. There we lay on the floor out of sight. The cars roared off, but we stayed put until dawn while Matthew sat by the front door, his shotgun in his lap.

I didn't know where to turn. I didn't feel I could trust any folk of authority in Drew. I had my husband drive me to Cleveland, the next town over, and I spoke to Mr. Moore, the head of the NAACP there. He notified the deputy sheriff of the county, and the FBI visited and took the bullets out of our walls as evidence. They promised there would be an investigation. But how would we sleep knowing someone wanted to do us harm?

The next night we returned to the back room, all of us huddled on the floor. I prayed and prayed for the Lord's covering. *Lord, keep my kids safe.* I also prayed, *Lord, help us eat.* That same day Matthew had gone to the country store, the only place we could buy on credit when we needed it. The manager took one look at my husband and said, "I'll give you until three o'clock to get your children out of the white school." When Matthew came home I dug out the 40 dollars I had saved under our mattress, so he could shop at another store. How much longer could we survive?

For four nights we slept in the back room, me worrying myself sick. Then one evening I recalled something I once heard a preacher say: "Everybody's afraid, and it's okay to be afraid, but you can't let fear stop you." No, I couldn't. And I wouldn't. People could complain and harass us all they wanted; we wouldn't be stopped. Like a blanket wrapped around each sleeping child, the covering of the Lord came over us. *Thank you, Lord,* I prayed. I slept better than I had in weeks, and the next night we returned to our bedrooms.

We worked hard preparing for the start of school. We picked cotton during the day, and in the evenings we readied the children's school clothes. No one would be able to say our children weren't neat and clean. Matthew had learned to sew from his mother; at night he made underwear for the girls out of flour sacks.

Help came from people we didn't even know. One day I was visiting friends down the road, and my daughter Beverly came running. "Mama," she said, "there's a white lady and a black lady waiting for you." Total strangers, they had heard about our situation. They said they were from New York and they were trying to help people like us. After taking plenty of notes and inspecting our bullet holes, they promised to tell our story and raise money from lodges, churches, synagogues and other groups up north.

But on September 3, 1965, the first day of school, after sending my kids off on the bus, I felt alone and afraid. I lay on the bed for hours, praying *Lord, keep my children safe.* When they finally burst through the door that afternoon I was so glad to see them again. I sat them down and made them tell me everything about their day. It hadn't been easy, but no way would they give up.

That fall I prayed every moment I could. Sometimes the children told me about being called "nigger" or having spitwads thrown at them. Once the bus driver told them to sit at the back of the bus, but they stayed up front. It broke my heart when Ruth told me one day, "I hate them. I hate those white folks."

"Ruth," I told her, "don't say that. Hate destroys you. Don't hate."

I could tell that Ruth was hurt. All fall Matthew and I continued to work in the fields, counting every penny we earned. As usual, we hoped to collect a few extra bales for ourselves by following behind the automatic picking machines. But that October, someone attached a disc to the tractor, which plowed the last of the cotton under. On December 10 the overseer told us we were 97 dollars in debt, and that there was no more land for us to work. We would have to move.

Even then I couldn't hate because the covering had come back. God was with us, and I knew in spite of everything we would be all right. We would find another place to live. We would find another way to earn a living. We had stepped out in faith and God would not let us down.

We moved into Drew, where Matthew got a job. From then on all our children attended Drew High School. Seven of them eventually graduated from Ole Miss.

A lot has changed since 1965. The world's a different place. These days people tell me I showed a lot of courage back then. I have to tell them it came with the Lord's covering. That's something that never changes.

WHAT DO THE LITTLE ONES SEE?

by Joan Wester Anderson

When my book *Where Angels Walk* was published in 1992, I was delighted by the positive response from readers. I had expected people to tell me about their own angel experiences, but I was surprised at how many parents wrote about their children's. One morning I settled down with a batch of mail and opened a typical letter. "You've done a lot of research on angels," a young mother wrote. "Have you ever heard of preschoolers seeing things we adults can't, or being aware of heaven and angels without anyone prompting them?"

Seeing things we can't . . . I recalled Peter, an imaginary companion my four sons had entertained many years ago. Peter hadn't "officially" lived with us, but frequently popped in to visit and to hear nightly prayers or share lunch. As an enlightened parent I had tolerated the boys' fantasy. "Is Peter here today?" I asked innocently. "Does he want a cookie?"

Now, as I read this letter, something occurred to me. No matter how impromptu my questions about Peter, my boys had always answered in unison. "No, Mommy," they said shaking their heads. "Peter didn't come today." Or if Peter was supposedly nearby, four pairs of eyes focused on the same spot in the room. "There he is—can't you see him?" one said, pointing while the others laughed. I had always taken it as a joke. Well, wasn't it?

During the next few weeks I asked my now-grown sons about Peter, and was rewarded with blank stares. No one recalled our game of pretend. Had it all been make-believe? And if so, why were other parents having the same kind of experience?

Nita Hannie, of Baton Rouge, Louisiana, wrote me about a difficult time when her son, Patrick, just turned two, was receiving chemotherapy as an outpatient. Patrick developed a low-grade fever, but instead of admitting him to the hospital, the emergency room physician prescribed an over-the-counter medicine. That evening Patrick's temperature rose. "I put him in bed with me, turned out the light and prayed about what to do," Nita recalls. "After maybe fifteen minutes of silence, Patrick suddenly sat up. Staring at a corner of the room, he said, 'Hi, angel!'"

"Patrick?" Nita whispered in the dark. "What are you seeing?"

Patrick didn't respond. "Hi, angel!" he repeated.

"He spoke with a comfort and familiarity usually reserved for family," Nita says. "He talked for nearly a minute in his own baby jabber, punctuated clearly with the word *angel,* then lay down, smiled at me and turned over to sleep." A half hour later Nita checked his temperature. Patrick was fever-free.

"Although Patrick has been back in the hospital since then, he continues to be in remission, and is doing well," Nita says. "I believe an angel was in the room with us, bringing healing and comfort, and Patrick saw it."

Patrick knew the word *angel.* Some children did not—yet their experiences were remarkably similar. When three-year-old Danny Agnese of Bethpage, New York, ran across the living room and tripped, his mother, Laura, watched in fear as he fell toward a sharp corner of a table. Suddenly Danny stopped in midair, righted himself and ran on, uninjured.

Laura was mystified. How could the law of gravity be defied? The next day Danny told her that he had seen "a pretty lady" in his room. "She caught me yesterday so I wouldn't hit my head against the table," he explained. "She said she would take care of me."

Danny had no formal knowledge of spiritual things; he had

seemed too young to learn. Then he saw a painting of an angel. "That's her!" he exclaimed. "That's the lady!"

These reports intrigued me. It seemed logical that children were closer to paradise than we adults—hadn't Jesus told us that their innocence and pure hearts were what the kingdom of God is all about? Perhaps little ones, so fresh from heaven, hadn't yet experienced a clear-cut boundary between the two worlds and for a short while could be part of both.

In addition to events happening to children today, I heard from many adults about their childhood experiences. "My parents must have let me out of their sight for a few moments. I remember wandering out to the neighboring highway, close to the center lane, then looking up, and seeing a huge truck coming down the hill toward me," recounted Marsha Wood of Maggie Valley, North Carolina. "There was something in front of the truck, like the sun's rays, with a shining figure in its center. I was much too young to understand then, but now I realize it was an angel that caused the truck to come to a complete stop, just inches from me."

Reverend Linda Walters, a pastor in Cheyenne, Wyoming, was seven when her younger cousin died of cancer. A few weeks later, she remembers, another little girl mysteriously arrived to play with her. The child did not attend Linda's school, and didn't seem to live nearby. But Linda was lonely, and accepted her new friend gratefully. The two played happily each day, but when Linda asked her mother for a snack to share, she got a surprise. Neither her mother, nor anyone else, could see the visitor.

"At first my mother was alarmed that I was having hallucinations, and she called the doctor," Linda reports. "He assured her that imaginary friends were normal, so the family played along with me."

The visitor came every day for several weeks, banishing Linda's sorrow. "Then one day she said she had to be moving along, that other people needed her help," Linda recalls. She never saw her friend again, but has never forgotten her.

These letters and others like them put things in a new light for me. Like Linda Walters's mother, I had assumed my sons' playmate was an illusion. After all, children do have rich imaginations, and not every story they tell is true. And yet, could mine have concocted such a perfectly timed practical joke, one that went on for several years before the veil between heaven and earth fully descended? What if Peter was more than just a pretend figure? What if he was a guardian angel?

I guess I'll never know for sure. But recently one of my sons told me about an evening when he was locked out of his truck. "I was in the back of a dark parking lot, miles from home, no stores open, and no way of getting the tool I needed to pop the lock," Bill explained. "Then, all of a sudden, another truck pulled in and drove right to where I was standing. The guy got out—carrying the tool I needed—sprung the lock, smiled at me, got in his truck and drove away." Bill looked at me. "What do you think of that, Mom?"

I think Peter is still on the job.

"Will You, Daddy?"

by Michael Foster

It's strange the things you remember when life has crumbled suddenly. It's not the important things that you remember—the plans of years; the love or hopes you've worked so hard for. It's the little things you had barely noticed: the way a little hand touched yours; the hopeful inflection of a voice.

John Carmody found that out, staring through the living room window at the cheerful Tuesday afternoon life on the street. He kept trying to think about the important things. But he couldn't get them focused in his mind.

All he could remember now was something his little girl had said to him one evening, two weeks ago. On that night, he had brought home from the office a draft of the annual stockholders' report. It was important to his family's future. He sat down to re-read it before dinner. It had to be right.

And just as he turned a page, Marge, his little girl, came with a book. It was a green-covered book, with a fairy-tale picture pasted on it. She said, "Look, Daddy."

He glanced up and said, "Oh, fine. A new book, eh?"

"Yes, Daddy," she said. "Will you read me a story in it?"

"No, dear. Not just now."

Marge just stood there as he read a paragraph that told the stockholders about replacements in the machinery of the factory. And Marge's voice, with hopeful inflection, was saying, "But Mummy said you probably would, Daddy."

He looked up. "I'm sorry," he answered. "Maybe Mummy will read it to you. I'm busy, dear."

"No," Marge said politely, "Mummy is much busier upstairs. Won't you read me one story?"

"Some other time."

After that, there was a long silence. Marge just stood there with the book open at a lovely picture. It was a long time before she said anything else.

He read through two more pages explaining the shift in markets, and plans for meeting these problems.

"But, Daddy, the story looks so exciting," Marge said.

"Some other time. Run along."

But Marge didn't go away. She stood quietly, like a good child. And after a long time, she put the book down at his feet and said, "Well, whenever you get ready, just read it to yourself. Only read it loud enough so I can hear."

"Sure," he said. "Sure—later."

And that was what John Carmody was remembering now, not the plans of love and care for the years ahead. He was remembering the way a well-mannered child had touched his hand with timid little fingers and said, "Just read it to yourself. Only read it loud enough so I can hear."

And that was why, now, he picked up the book and opened it to the lovely picture.

And reading the story, his lips moving stiffly with anguish to form the words, he didn't try to think about the important things, about his plans for the years to come. And for a little while, he forgot, even, his hate for the drunken driver who had careened down the street in a car, and who was now in jail on manslaughter charges.

He didn't even see his wife—white and silent—dressed to be with Marge for the last time, standing in the doorway, trying to make her voice say calmly, "I'm ready, dear. We must go."

Because John Carmody was reading:

> Once upon a time, there was a little girl who lived in a wood-cutter's hut, in the Black Forest. And she was so fair that the birds forgot their singing from the bough, looking at her. And there came a day when . . . .

He was reading it to himself. But loud enough for Marge to hear.

The Boat That Brought Daddy Home

by Bonnie Harris

When I was growing up, Aunt Faith and Uncle Clinton's cottage on Live Oak Island, in the Gulf of Mexico, was my second home. Every summer weekend Mama and Daddy piled my younger sister, my baby brother and me into our blue-and-white Oldsmobile and drove the twenty miles from Tallahassee, Florida, armed with bathing suits, Pecan Sandies and jugs of drinking water that sloshed about as we headed down the sandy road in the middle of the tiny isle.

The minute we pulled up to the cottage, my sister and I jumped out and raced to the dock to find our cousins. Using bacon bits for bait, we fished for hours, catching shiners. At low tide we scoured the beach for scallop shells, sea urchins and other treasures. Evenings we drafted a newspaper, which we painstakingly copied by hand and sold to the neighbors for a quarter.

I loved Live Oak Island for all the good times I had there with my cousins, even for the sunburns and writer's cramp. I loved it even more, though, for the way it seemed to change my parents. Back home on the mainland they were strict and serious, especially Daddy. He was the head of boat registration for the State Conservation

Service, and was often too tired after a long day of work to horse around with us. As soon as we crossed the bridge to Live Oak, his worries seemed to waft away on the island breeze. Out at the beach cottage I felt I got to see Daddy the way he really was: a fun-loving, down-to-earth guy who liked nothing better in life than serving fish hot off the grill and leading us kids on crabbing expeditions.

One Saturday morning when I was nine, Daddy, Uncle Clinton and a friend of my uncle's decided to take my boy cousins, Bobby and Donnie, grouper fishing by Buoy 24, an hour's boat ride away. My sister and I and our girl cousins stayed on the island. We slipped into bathing suits and smeared on globs of Coppertone, ready for a day in the sun. We fished off the dock a while, even caught some blue crabs on our lines. Then we went to the beach. The tide was dead low, and we played hopscotch on the hot sand.

There was a thunderstorm late in the afternoon, so all the fishing boats came in early. All the boats, that is, except Daddy's. We waited and waited. When Mama started pacing up and down, I knew something was dreadfully wrong. The shortwave radio blared as the afternoon turned into evening. Six o'clock, then seven o'clock . . . still no boat. And no Daddy.

Mama called the U.S. Coast Guard and the Florida marine patrol. Some of our neighbors joined the search. Darkness fell. I felt alone and afraid. Daddy always got home before dark. What if he was never coming back?

I wandered the beach. Usually I liked watching the moonlight play on the waves, but that night its reflection on the water seemed a cruel reminder of the miles of ocean standing between me and my father.

I walked back to the cottage. My mother was sitting on the porch steps, head in her hands. "Mama, is there any news?" I asked softly.

She looked up, desperation rimming her eyes, and struggled to find something hopeful to say. "The Coast Guard and marine patrol are positive they'll find them soon."

"Do you believe that?"

"I have to," Mama managed before she burst into tears.

I put my arms around her. "I know they'll find them, Mama," I said, wanting to believe it too. "Please don't cry."

She nodded and slipped out of my embrace. She wanted to be

alone, so I decided to go up to bed. As I shut the porch door behind me, I could hear her desperate murmur, "Please, Lord, bring them home safe," drift through the screen. Before I got into bed I stood at the window, staring out to sea and added my own prayer to Mama's: *God, please take care of Daddy and Uncle Clinton and his friend and the cousins, wherever they are.*

We were eating breakfast in silence the next morning when the shortwave radio crackled. Mama leaned close to the speaker. I saw joy spread across her face. "They found them!" she cried. "They're taking them to Spring Creek right now. Quick, get in the car!" My sister and I hopped in the Oldsmobile with my baby brother. Mama got in, and we sped down the sandy road and crossed the bridge to the mainland, Aunt Faith and the girls following in their car.

Minutes later we stood at the end of the dock in Spring Creek, anxiously watching for the boat that was bringing Daddy and the rest back. "There they are!" Jumping up and down, we clapped and waved as the boat approached. It belonged to Lynell Spears, a man from Spring Creek who made his living fishing in the Gulf.

First Bobby and Donnie jumped onto the dock. Then Uncle Clinton and his friend—and finally, Daddy, his red plaid cap perched on top of his head. He looked tired, but a huge grin split his sunburned face. We enveloped him in hugs. "What happened?" Mama asked. She stepped back to look him over head to toe, her no-nonsense self returning now that the crisis was over. "And why do you have a bloody shirt tied around your waist?"

"You'll never believe it," Daddy said. "The motor exploded when we got to Buoy 24, and the boat sank. We tied ourselves together in a ring, using our life jackets, and drifted with the tide for hours. The boys got so thirsty they tried to drink the saltwater. Schools of sharks and barracuda started swimming around us. One of the sharks came so close its fin cut my belly. I used my shirt to stop the bleeding." He paused to take a deep breath.

"That's enough talking," Mama decided. "You need rest."

"But I haven't gotten to the best part," Daddy

protested. "Late at night we finally drifted onto a sandbar, where the water was only chest-deep. Still, we couldn't risk falling asleep and being swept back out to sea. Clinton and I kept nudging the cousins and talking to keep from dropping off. I didn't want to say it in front of the boys, but I had just about given up hope that we'd ever be rescued."

"Oh, Daddy!" I exclaimed, remembering how alone I'd felt and knowing he must have felt a thousand times worse.

"Then Bobby said he saw a tugboat," Daddy continued. "Sure enough, far away on the horizon, there it was—the unmistakable outline of a tugboat, its big round light raking a path in the darkness."

"Did they come and get you?" my sister asked.

"Not exactly," Daddy said. "Bobby asked me, 'C'mon, don't you see the angel on the bow?' As hard as I tried, I couldn't see it. But Bobby was convinced, and all of us on the fishing boat believed him. Even after the tugboat disappeared over the horizon, we weren't worried. I wasn't sure how, but I knew I'd see y'all again.

"Just a few hours later Lynell appeared out of nowhere. I asked him how in the world he had found us. He told me he'd envisioned the five of us on a particular sandbar in the Gulf. So he headed straight to the spot. There we were!"

"With the Coast Guard and the marine patrol all searching, a fisherman is the one who finds you. . . . " Mama said, shaking her head. "It's a miracle."

"Don't I know it," Daddy agreed. "There's no doubt in my mind God put that angel on the tugboat to let us know he was looking out for us. I bet that same angel told Lynell exactly where to go."

That night, back at the cottage, I thought about what Daddy had said. Only God could have found a way to take care of us all: hearing Mama's and my prayers; reassuring Daddy and the others while they were lost at sea; and sending to their rescue a fisherman who knew the Gulf waters like the back of his own hand.

Forty years later that knowledge still sustains me. So does Live Oak Island. I visit often. I love it more now than I did when I was little. For it was there that God taught me my first lesson in miracles. And it is there—on the beach, watching the sunlight dappling the waves, the sand warm between my toes—that I still feel closest to Him.

Teen For A Day

by Karen Barber

We had just moved and I was dropping off my tenth grader, Chris, at his school. I was ready to leave, but he wasn't. Chris's brown bangs flopped across his forehead as he jerked away in annoyance. "Mom, we're leaving too early. You just don't understand!"

Tension crept into my neck. Now that Chris was a teenager, at times I felt like I was attempting to communicate with a being from another planet and not with the fun-loving offspring I had been raising for the past 15 years. "What is there to understand?" I shot back. "In case there's traffic we need to leave at 7:45."

"I can't hang around all by myself before the bell," Chris mumbled.

"We're not risking being late for such a ridiculous reason," I answered. We left promptly at 7:45 A.M.

The following week Chris staggered in from school and dumped his backpack with a thump that made me frown. When I asked him about his classes, it became clear he hadn't been participating in class discussions. "Chris," I argued, "you have good ideas."

"But none of the other kids say anything."

So what? I wrinkled my forehead. Maybe I was the one who just wasn't getting it. *Why won't a smart kid speak up in class?*

That weekend I overheard Chris telling his brother he had shoved someone in the halls. "Chris!" I horned in. "How could you do such a thing?"

"You don't know how crowded it is," he protested. "The guy was in my way and he was just standing there talking to somebody."

"Don't ever do that again!" I scolded. Chris turned and stomped off to his room. As his stereo blasted I prayed, *Lord, what does it take to understand a teenager?*

The first week in October I received a notice about the school's "Wacky Tuesday." Parents were invited to attend school in place of their teenagers and the teenagers were to go to their parents' place of work. There were rules: Each parent had to stay for the entire day and take notes for his or her child. Apparently, several dozen parents did it every year. It sounded interesting, so I signed up.

The day before Wacky Tuesday, I told Chris, "This afternoon when I pick you up I want you to show me how to find all your classes."

"No way, Mom. Nobody showed me around the first day. I want you to know exactly how I felt."

"Fine," I answered, thinking. *What on earth has gotten into him?*

On Wacky Tuesday, Chris put on a shirt and a tie and went to the office with my husband, Gordon. I pulled on a turtleneck, slacks and running shoes. I heaved a backpack crammed with Chris's books over my shoulders, and was off to high school at a quarter to eight.

Inside the school with time to spare and no one to talk to, I stood uncomfortably, listing under the weight of the backpack.

Okay, I'd try to make sense of the map the school had given out. I had to get to room 5109, placed for some reason on the first level.

I plunged into a traffic jam of students, gym duffels, and open lockers and turned down the wrong hall. I raced to correct my course and found the stairway blocked by a girl with a gargantuan book bag. As the girl prattled mindlessly with some friends, I thought, *This kid is as effective a roadblock as a hippopotamus.* I elbowed my way through oncoming traffic, not bothering to say excuse me as I rushed.

In Algebra II the teacher handed out a graded exam and went through the solutions on the blackboard. She wrote so fast I could barely copy the figures down. It was a scene from a nightmare: I walk into an exam and haven't the foggiest notion how to do anything.

The knot in my stomach tightened during second and third periods. In Geography the kids working on our project responded to my suggestions with blank stares. In Keyboarding, the lesson was on keys I rarely used.

Lunch was next. There were several empty places, but I hesitated. *What if they're saving those places for their friends? Or don't want me around?* Finally I spotted a bunch of parents and practically sprinted to an empty spot at their table.

I had been looking forward to English, and had eagerly read the assigned pages in *Lord of the Flies*. The teacher asked the class how they envisioned the forest fire the boys carelessly start. *Such details don't matter; the book is more of a parable than a news account,* I wanted to say. For some reason my hand stayed firmly by my side. *Maybe the teacher is about to make that point and I'd steal his thunder. Or maybe I'll sound show-offy or stupid and the others will laugh at me.*

Biology was my last class, and it was lab day. We frantically measured and cut straws into various lengths to represent differing ionization rates. The final bell rang just when I read the rather odd last question on the lab sheet: "What did you learn about yourself in this lab?"

I gathered my books and plunged into the frantic hall. *I'm not fighting those hippopotamuses through the crowded halls just to stash these in Chris's locker,* I decided. Instead, I fled out the nearest exit.

My car was parked three blocks away. By the second block the backpack straps cut into my shoulders and my lower back was screaming out that I was, after all, a middle-aged woman. When I walked through the kitchen door and threw down that book bag, I felt a thousand pounds lighter. *So this is how Chris feels when he gets home.*

Suddenly I found myself mentally filling in that last question on the biology lab sheet. I had done everything I had been criticizing Chris for. At lunch I had dreaded sitting with strangers. In English class I had kept quiet. And in my panic to get to class on time I had done some aggressive pushing.

When Chris got home from his dad's office he looked at his stuffed book bag and groaned. "Don't tell me I have that much homework!"

"You don't," I explained sheepishly. "I didn't feel like fighting the hippopotamuses to get to your locker." "High school's hard work. I'm glad I got to see what you have to deal with."

"Yep." Chris' nonchalant shrug could mean "typical parent, stating the obvious again." But I could see the shrug went along with a look in his eye that meant my fun-loving offspring was communicating, "Well, Mom finally gets it."

I grinned. Yes, I finally "got" not just my teenager, but also what the Book of Proverbs has been teaching parents for thousands of years: "Be ye of an understanding heart" (Proverbs 8:5).

GRANDMA HITA

by Cynthia Brooks

When I was nine years old the thought of death petrified me. I could not stand the prospect of anyone close to me being taken away, nor could I face the eternal emptiness that I feared was death. Dead. The very word sent me into panic.

One evening, about a year after the birth of my sister, my father announced that my mom's mother, Grandma Hita, was moving in with us. (I called her Grandma Hita because she always called me *mi jita*—her shortened version of *mi hijita*—"my little child" in Spanish.) Dad explained that Grandma's failing health did not allow her to live alone any longer. My heart raced and I felt dizzy. Grandma Hita was old and might *die* while she was with us!

But after Grandma moved into the baby's room, everything seemed to be all right. Grandma's presence calmed us all. She shuffled quietly throughout the house and was glad to do laundry, press shirts, start dinner and mend dresses. And every night she sat on the edge of her bed and changed the bandages on her badly ulcerated leg sores.

"How did you get those sores, Grandma?" I asked one night. In her broken English she told me that she had been pregnant most of her childbearing years—21 times! Even though only six of her children had survived, the pregnancies had been hard on her body, and her legs in particular. But she never complained.

I got used to wandering into Grandma's room and talking with her as she mended a blouse or wrote a birthday card to one of her other grandchildren. I loved to lie on her bed and visit with her. She became my closest confidant, and I went to her with many of my problems.

One Saturday morning my mother left me a long list of chores. I was not allowed to go out and play until every job was crossed off the list. "How am I going to do all of this?" I whined.

Grandma Hita spoke softly, "I help you, and little by little, *mi jita,* we get it all done."

I noticed Grandma's lips moving while we worked. "What are you doing, Grandma?" I asked.

"I pray to the Lord, *mi jita,*" she said. "God will help us do our work."

Another day I came running home in tears. I was 11; Kathy, another neighborhood girl, had just told me the family I had been baby-sitting for regularly had asked her to baby-sit the next Saturday night. I cried in Grandma's lap as I questioned why the family I loved so much would drop me so abruptly. I tried so hard to be the best baby-sitter ever, bathing the three little boys and reading them bedtime stories. I had thought I was appreciated, but now my heart was broken.

Grandma brushed my hair away from my face and whispered, "Don't worry, *mi jita,* justice wins out in the end. Jesus knows what is in your heart. He take care of everything." But I had a hard time believing her.

The next morning, Dale, the mother of the boys, called and asked me to come over. I walked the block to her house petulant and hurt. Was she going to tell me Kathy would be their regular baby-sitter? But when we sat down Dale placed a pearl ring in my hand. "This belonged to my mother. Since I have no daughters, I want you to have it. You have become such a part of our family that we want you to know how much we love you." She invited me to attend the mother-daughter banquet with her at her church on Saturday night. So that's why she had asked Kathy to baby-sit! Grandma had been right again.

As the days turned into years Grandma became an integral part of our family, and insisted on helping in every way possible. She mended my sister Helen's cheerleading skirt and stitched my brother Kenny's pants. My baby sister, Mary Anne, often took her nap in Grandma's arms.

One evening as I sat on the edge of her bed, I choked out, "Grandma, I don't ever want you to die."

Instead of recoiling in horror, she laughed out loud. "Oh, *mi jita,* you don't mean that. I am so tired. I looking forward to no more sore legs. I looking forward to seeing Jesus and resting in His arms."

"But I'll miss you so much!" I cried.

"Oh, no, *mi jita,* I'm never going to leave you." I looked into her eyes and could not believe what I saw. She was so old and close to death and yet she was happy to talk about it. She held me tight and continued to chuckle.

I watched Grandma closely and noticed how often she prayed. Not just at church or before bed but almost constantly. I too prayed for the serenity Grandma felt about death.

The weekend of my aunt and uncle's twenty-fifth wedding anniversary approached. Early in the week Grandma went to stay with them in Anaheim to help prepare for the festivities. Mom, Dad, Mary Anne and I traveled to the church on Saturday morning for the anniversary Mass. We waited excitedly until my aunt and uncle finally appeared and walked down the aisle to the wedding march. But as they neared our pew I could see my aunt's face was puffy from crying. As she approached she leaned over to my mother and said, "Mama's just had a stroke. She's in the hospital."

I barely remember the next two days except that there were constant comings and goings to and from the hospital. I wasn't allowed to visit—Grandma wasn't conscious, I was told—and I kept myself busy trying to entertain four-year-old Mary Anne.

A few days later I woke in the morning to see my dad sitting on my bed. "Grandma died just a little while ago," he whispered. I hugged my dad, and as I did, instead of being engulfed by the fear and panic I had always expected and dreaded, I felt a surprising peace and calm. Death had happened. My grandmother, whom I loved intensely, had died. But I knew she was where she wanted to be. That night I slept better than I ever had.

I am grown now and have a child of my own. And there are still times I long to lie on Grandma Hita's lap. I miss her. But when my daughter is overwhelmed by a pile of homework, I tell her "Little by little, *mi jita.*" Or when my husband laments injustice at his workplace, I say, "Don't worry, Honey, justice wins out in the end. Jesus knows what's in your heart." I feel again the gentle peace I knew when I nestled in Grandma Hita's lap. And I smile, knowing Grandma is indeed still with me—and we are both resting where we belong.

"These Are the Children We Hold Dear"

by Jacqui Kess-Gardner

From the way my pregnancy had gone, there was no sign of anything wrong with the baby. I took care of myself, ate lots of fruit and vegetables, did my stretching exercises. I had every expectation things would go as smoothly as they had when my first son, Jamaal, was born. An easy delivery and a perfect child.

But that May day, when I was in the delivery room, squeezing my husband's hand as we heard our baby's first cry, the nurse lifted the boy up in a receiving blanket and exclaimed, "Mrs. Gardner, something is wrong here!" The doctor shot her an angry glance. I looked in horror as the nurse pulled back the blanket to show us our son. One eye was sealed shut. The other was a milky mass. He had no bridge to his nose and his face looked crushed. Although I knew I should take him in my arms and hold him, I couldn't. I just couldn't. The nurse whisked him away and a few minutes later I was wheeled to the recovery room.

There I lay, the curtain pulled around me. My husband James had gone to make some calls. On the other side of the curtain I could hear other new mothers whispering to their babies, cooing as they coaxed them to nurse. I even heard one mother complain to her husband, "Not another boy," and I was so filled with a jealous rage that I almost trembled. *God,* I prayed, *why have You done this to us?* I was furious.

I thought of all the dreams I had had for this child: How I would cuddle up with him and read from brightly colored picture books, his finger idly tracing the page; how I had hoped he would sing or paint or play the piano like his older brother, his eyes studying the keys. Instead, my baby was blind and painful to look at. I was in shock.

Slowly, deliberately, I walked to the phone and dialed my mom. She was home taking care of Jamaal. My agony and confusion poured out between sobs: "It's a boy. His eyes won't open. His face is deformed. I don't think I can handle this. What am I going to do, Mom?"

My question hung in the air. Then Mom said in quiet, measured tones, "You will bring him home. These are the children we hold dear. Bring him home and nurture him."

After I hung up, the postpartum nurse led me to a private room. I sank down on the sofa, my mother's words echoing in my head, *These are the children we hold dear.*

"Nurse," I said, "I need to fix myself up." I unzipped my flowered cosmetic case and took out a comb and my brightest lipstick. In my suitcase I found my green satin robe and gold high-heeled slippers. I sprayed on my favorite perfume. Maybe my son couldn't see me, but I wanted to look my best for him.

I made my way down the polished hospital corridor, past the brightly lit newborn nursery to a darker room where special cases were kept. The incubators seemed like tiny space capsules tethered to flashing green screens. Machines whirred and whooshed softly. A nurse appeared at my side and led me to a rocker. "Sit here, Mrs. Gardner," she said. "I'll bring him to you."

She placed a small, blanketed bundle in my arms. Taking a deep breath, I looked down at my son. I had hoped he would look different. But he didn't. His forehead protruded. Under the sealed eyelid the eyeball was missing. The other was spaced far from it. His bridgeless nose was bent to the side of his face. The doctors called it hypertelorism. I didn't know what to call it.

But even as anger at God surged through me I began to see

things I liked about this baby. He had beautiful black curly hair. His tiny mouth was like a perfect rosebud. His skin was silky. I moved my finger into his soft brown palm and his long and tapered fingers closed around it. Gently I unwrapped him. Except for the face he was perfect in every way. He turned his head and nuzzled. I opened the green satin robe and soon he was nursing.

As we rocked I began to talk to him. "Hello, Jermaine," I said. "That's your name. I am your mommy and I love you. I'm sorry I waited so long to come. Please forgive me. You have a big brother and a wonderful father who love you too.

"I promise to work hard to make your life the best it can be. Your grandpa had a lovely voice and could play the piano and sing. So what if you can't see? I can give you music. That I can do."

Over the next few months, my husband and I poured our energies into filling up the darkness in Jermaine's life. One of us carried him in his Snugli or backpack at all times. We talked and sang to him constantly. We inundated him with music, mostly classical interspersed with some Lionel Richie and Stevie Wonder. Four-year-old Jamaal was already taking piano lessons and when he practiced I sat next to him on the piano bench with his little brother in my lap.

But I still couldn't let go of my anger. I wouldn't go to church. I stopped reading the Bible. I hardly ever prayed. Because I couldn't stand anyone staring at my baby, I avoided going out of the house. I didn't want to hear people's comments. What really hurt was not getting any smiles from Jermaine, which is common in blind infants—they can't mimic a smile because they don't see anyone smiling at them. But it felt like another slight from God.

Every day my younger sister Keetie called me. "Jacqui," she said, "you've got to pray to God to forgive you. You've got to come back to him. He has a plan." Still I resisted.

Then one day when Jermaine was six months old, my sister called me while I was fixing dinner. The baby was strapped to my back, toying with my hair. Music blared from the stereo. Cradling the phone between shoulder and ear, I stirred the spaghetti sauce. And for some reason I found myself crying. I put the spoon down and repeated the words Keetie was praying, "Lord, forgive me. I have been angry at You. I'm sorry. Help me trust in Your wisdom. I know You have some plan in this. Help me see it."

"Hallelujah!" Keetie shouted.

Two months later God's plan was revealed. Jamaal had been practicing the piano in the family room, playing "Lightly Row" again and again. (By then I had taken to leaving Jermaine strapped to his high chair next to the piano while his brother played.) He had just finished, and came downstairs to the bedroom where James and I were sitting. Suddenly a familiar *plink plunk-plunk, plink plunk-plunk* floated down the stairs. I looked at James; James looked at me. It couldn't be Jamaal. He was jumping on the bed in front of us. We stared at each other for a second, then tore upstairs.

At the piano, his head thrown back, a first-ever smile splitting his face, Jermaine was playing "Lightly Row." The right keys, the right rhythm. It was extraordinary.

"Thank you, Jesus!" I cried, and gave Jermaine a huge hug. James ran to the phone to call almost everybody we knew. In the next hour the house filled up. I sat Jermaine at the piano in his high chair and we stood around expectantly. Nothing happened. I hummed "Lightly Row" and played a few notes. Jermaine sat silent, his hands motionless.

"It was just a fluke," James said.

"No," I said, "it couldn't have been." Our eight-and-a-half-month-old son had perfectly replicated a tune.

One morning two weeks later as I was washing dishes, he did it again, this time playing another piece Jamaal had practiced. Dripping suds, I ran into the family room and stood listening as the notes became firmer and the tune melded into its correct form. Jermaine had found the incredible gift God had given him.

There was no stopping him. He demanded to be at the piano from morning until bedtime. Often I fed him there, wiping strained applesauce off the keys as I thanked God. At first he only played Jamaal's practice songs, then he played Lionel Richie's "Hello" after hearing it on the tape recorder. At 18 months he played the left-hand part of Beethoven's "Moonlight Sonata" while my sister played the right-hand. When he gave his first concerts I crawled under the piano to work the foot pedals for him.

By the time he was out of diapers I was desperate to find him a good teacher. I heard about a man at the Maryland School for the Blind and called him. I explained that Jermaine was already playing the piano. “How old is he?” the teacher asked.

“Two and a half.”

“A child that age is too young to start,” he said disapprovingly, just as strains of the “Moonlight Sonata” filtered in from the other room. “By the way, Mrs. Gardner, who is that playing in the background?”

“That’s my son!”

“Bring him in!”

Soon invitations for Jermaine to perform came from far and wide. He appeared on national television. He played for two first ladies in the White House, and Stevie Wonder asked him to play with him at his studio in California. Thanks to a pair of Texas philanthropists who saw Jermaine on TV he was flown to Dallas, where he had special surgery to rebuild his face. Now with his dark glasses on, he looks like any 13-year-old kid.

Today he attends a public school and excels in reading Braille, math and spelling. He has added clarinet to his repertoire. He says that when he grows up he would like to start a music school for the blind.

One afternoon recently I watched Jermaine play a few selections for friends. He had come downstairs barefoot, his long legs protruding from green Bermuda shorts. As his fingers flew across the keys I thought of my sister Keetie’s words. God had a plan for our son. He did indeed.

Pitch and Catch

by Fred Bauer

Incline your ear, and come unto me:
hear, and your soul shall live....
— Isaiah 55:3

I have noticed that when conversation between two people is sparse, it helps to give their hands an occupation. Men seem to talk easier when holding fishing poles, for example. And I imagine words flow easier for women when they're working together on a business report at lunch or sharing ideas for a church potluck.

Whenever I want to have a deep discussion with one of my three sons, we go to the backyard and play catch. I doubt that the founder of baseball, Alexander Cartwright, had any idea that this game would prove such a boon to father-son relationships, but others confirm its contribution. A career decision was troubling one of my guys recently, and when I sensed his struggle, I gathered gloves and ball and led him out beneath the spreading maple where our game of catch is always played. For a long time neither of us said much of anything. The only sound was that of ball hitting leather—*smack, smlat, smack, smlat.* Eventually, his concerns surfaced, and between *smacks* and *smlats* I got a few reassuring *uh-huhs* and *yeps.*

Soon, Shirley called us in for dinner. Nothing had been resolved by the ballplayers, yet I could tell by my son's body language and from the expression on his face that he felt better. It reminded me of the feeling I get when, confused and uncertain, I bare my soul to my heavenly Father. I don't always come away from those conversations with every care answered, but the fact that He hears my prayers is usually enough to dampen my doubts and reassure me that tomorrow will be a brand-new ball game.

School me, Lord, in the art of listening for Your Word,
Buttoning my lip until Your voice is heard.

More Than One Mom

by Candace Purdom

Mother's Day is a big deal for Terry, of suburban Chicago. He sends cards to all *three* of his moms.

There's the mom who adopted him. Later his adoptive parents divorced, and now he has a stepmom who married his dad. Then there's the mom who gave birth to him. As Terry, 15, explains, "The more the merrier."

Out of five kids in Terry's family, two are adopted. And like lots of adopted kids, Mother's Day leaves them feeling a little different.

Tons of kids have stepparents, but not so many are adopted. Even fewer have the kind of open relationship Terry and his birth mother have. After years of questions, and with his mom's help, Terry met his birth mom when he was 10.

"I feel lucky. Now I can call her up and say, 'Happy Mother's Day,'" Terry says. "But before I met her, I would keep asking my mom, 'What's her name?' 'What's she look like?' 'Do you have any pictures of her?'"

Wondering is totally normal for adopted kids. But all the mushy commercials and cards at this time of year may make those feelings harder to handle.

"Adopted kids do think about their birth parents—not every day or every hour, but some of the time," says Chicago-area therapist Nancy Golden. "When Mother's Day rolls around, that's going to stir up kids' feelings about having a birth mom and an adopted mom. There's nothing wrong with feeling that way."

When adopted kids are clueless about their birth parents, Golden suggests talking to their parents or other adopted kids about their feelings. Some kids even honor their birth mother with a Mother's Day candle-lighting ceremony.

After all, honoring your mother—or mothers—is really what Mother's Day is all about.

INDEX

A Note from the Editors

This original Guideposts book was created by the book division of the company that publishes *Guideposts, Plus, Positive Living, Guideposts for Kids* and *Angels on Earth*. Each magazine contains faith-filled true stories to help the reader live a more fulfilled life.

For more than twenty years, the book division has edited the annual devotional book *Daily Guideposts*, which contains new devotionals every year to inspire and uplift.

If you are interested in subscribing to any of the Guideposts family of publications, all you have to do is write Guideposts, 39 Seminary Hill Road, Carmel, NY 10512.

Guideposts is also available on the Internet. Send prayer requests to our Monday morning Prayer Fellowship. Share in praying for other readers. Read stories from recent issues of our magazines or read today's devotional from *Daily Guideposts*. Excerpts from some of our bestselling books are also available. **http://www.guideposts.org.**